C000008725

PRAISE FOR

A Quest for Identity

"With honesty and courage, Parastu Ahang Mehdawi tells her story of leaving Afghanistan, struggling to establish herself in Germany, and eventually rebuilding her life in Canada. Ultimately the story about searching for one's voice and place in the world—I rooted for her every step of the way!"

MARCIA WALKER, AUTHOR

"*No one had ever asked me about myself before, who I am as a person, as a woman. What did it mean, my happiness, my dreams, my longings?*" This is the story of the author's long journey to find herself. She unveils her life as a teenager in war-torn Afghanistan as she searches for who she is now. From Afghanistan to Prague and Paris, from Germany to Canada, we travel with her as she finds her way through life.

I was intrigued right from the start – *A Quest for Identity*. I wanted to know about this woman and where her story was going. As the story moved through the years, I was drawn into her world and felt that I was right beside her as she remembered her past. Her fears, confusion and happiness became mine. She drew me not only into her real world but also into the world of the young girl inside.

I read about hope, fear, and her passion for literature and poetry. The book shares the thoughts of a teen moving forward unsure what the future holds. It is a story about a refugee finding her way in the world. It is her "lifelong affair to be somebody."

PATRICIA BAILEY, AUTHOR

A QUEST

FOR IDENTITY

A QUEST
FOR IDENTITY

FROM AFGHANISTAN TO THE WORLD

PARASTU AHANG MEHDAWI

A Quest for Identity: From Afghanistan to the World

Copyright ©2022, Parastu Ahang Mehdawi

All rights reserved. No portion of this book may be reproduced in any form without permission from the publisher, except as permitted by Canadian copyright law. For permissions contact: paramehdawi@hotmail.com or visit www.ParastuaMehdawi.com

To ensure confidentiality, some names have been changed.

ISBN: 978-1-7782313-0-8 (Trade Paperback)
ISBN: 978-1-7782313-2-2 (Hard Cover)
ISBN: 978-1-7782313-1-5 (eBook)

Edited by: Marcia Walker

Copy Editor: Susan Gaigher

Front Cover Photography: Cynthia Summer

Cover Design and Interior Layout: Becky's Graphic Design®, LLC

BeckysGraphicDesign.com

To my sons Yuseuf, who taught me that I too could have a dream and chase it, and Elias, who stood tall beside me and said, "Mom, finish your book first."

To Frau Bors, who pulled back my voice before it could decay inside of me.

Contents

Preface

*"I do not know where I am going,
but I am on my way."*

—VOLTAIRE

Where would I be living now if I had been born in a land where the break of dawn was not met by exploding bombs? Where dusk did not promise to hide the cold bodies on the side of the road, and peace was not just a dream? Who would I have become if I had known who I was earlier in my journey? Would I now be an author with a voice, speaking up for fundamental human rights?

I journeyed to my past, and we spoke and cried on the shoulder of circumstance. I probed, peeled off the skin of my degraded history, and freed the genuine me.

Life turned a new page, and I walked on the path that I had dreamed of for decades. Since then, I have been waking up at dawn to feed my hunger for knowledge by reading articles on literature. First-person narratives cradled me and whispered, you are home. I googled to find the best memoirs and autobiographies of all time, and I read most of them. One article led to another, one video to another, and I embraced information from all around the globe—all just a click away. I joined Audible and downloaded it to my phone. I took long walks with authors while they told me their stories, and I became enlightened.

Every day, as the arts and artists encircled me, I felt that I belonged. I moved on to Nobel Prize-winning works of literature. Researching the winners' names produced a swarm of articles on a variety of subjects. I kept my head down and scrolled through the pages.

I read Elie Wiesel's acceptance speech for the Noble Prize in 1986 several times, and I cried.

Winning the 2018 Nobel Prize, Doctor Denis Mukwege mentioned the disgrace of human action. I cried.

Nadia Murad, another Nobel Prize winner, screamed about genocide. I cried.

In 2015, Yeonmi Park spoke of the search for freedom. Again, I cried.

I wadded up tissues soaked in tears.

On August 15th, 2021, early in the humid morning, my breath coiled inside my throat. I panted for air. I got up from my bed to open the window. The air was striking. The sun, just returned from the northeastern hemisphere, looked mysterious.

I compelled the sun to name his sorrow. He replied, "I am saddened by a nation in terror this morning." He continued as he climbed into the air, "In their despair to free themselves, I saw a crowd hanging onto the arms of an airplane.

Mothers abandoned their children in the hands of Western soldiers and pleaded for their safety.

Like a herd of sheep in the airport, people begged the Western world to grant them fundamental human rights."

He proceeded, "Alas, when I arrived at the tip of the horizon, I saw everything.

People fled the capital on foot, leaving their homes in fear for their safety. Women once again imprisoned themselves in the walls of their homes to survive.

I saw the moon moaning as she left, biting her lips in dismay. I stood puzzled to see the Dark Ages return twenty years into the 21st century."

He cried, "Afghanistan, the name of the place I speak of is Afghanistan."

I shouted, "Enough! Enough, I was born there."

Once, I was a teenager who survived the bloodshed of that troubled land, a girl who lived in a male-dominated region. As an adolescent, I heard stories that parents sold their children to survive hunger. The cry of a neighbor's daughter, who was too embarrassed to go to school because she had torn sandals, still resonates in my ears.

I crossed the oceans in search of a better life. Years passed. A belief grew in me that history would not repeat itself in the age of technology and reason. Humanity would not allow that agony again.

Yet, as I wake up to freedom, millions around the globe wake up to modern slavery, world hunger, war, and genocide.

The pen in my hand moves. I stand before everyone who faces misery caused by humankind and utter, I hear you.

I found my voice, and I have a platform, but how can I be heard? Can I tell you my story first?

Parastu Ahang Mehdawi
May 2022

Chapter One

"My name is Parastu Ahang Mehdawi."

I wrote in the notebook, and then I stopped. I tried to make sense of the challenging question raised by Yuseuf. I took a sip of my coffee and returned to my thoughts.

Who is Parastu?

With both arms on the table, I rested my head on clenched fists. My eyes fixated on the window as I sat at the end of the coffee shop. I loved this seat for its privacy, view, and wall socket for my computer. The parking lot, in between the coffee shop and other stores, was filled with cars. The driver and passengers of each car authored various hidden stories. The glass entry door led customers to the coffee bar that divided the store in two. On the right, seats leaned against the wall. On the left, three large glass windows homed four booths.

The sky dressed in layers of clouds while golden rays shined on the plaza. The mountain, with a snowcap on its head, stood tall. The trees danced in the breeze and carpeted the ground with amber, scarlet, and cinnamon leaves. The beauty of the Earth took me aback. I raised my head, taking another sip of coffee. It ran to the depths of my spirit.

The echo of Yuseuf's question invaded my whole body, and I couldn't free myself without reflection.

"Mom, what are you going to do with the time you have on your hands? What do you like? What has your heart ever desired that you never had the chance nor the time to pursue? Mom, what makes you happy?"

My eyes watered with remorse. No one had ever asked me about myself before, who I am as a person, as a woman. What did it mean, my happiness, my dreams, my longings? I felt a sudden jolt of power in my hands. For once in my life, I had the freedom to do whatever my heart desired.

What do I want in life? What are my desires? What makes me happy? Who am I?

＊＊

ON DECEMBER 7ᵀᴴ of 1988, I woke to see the dark night morphing into a dull orange, a new day that bruised my emotions. I glanced around. Nothing looked familiar. I wasn't used to waking up in this room. It was a small, narrow space. On the walls was a light beige wallpaper printed with brown flowers. On the floor, a mattress where my oldest brother, Arash, was sleeping. Above the bed was a window overlooking a fine lawn where large trees, planted in rows of three, grew in the winter cold.

I lay motionless on the bed, eyes pinned to the ceiling, reminiscing, as tears rolled into my hair. I forced my thoughts to recall how I wound up here. It felt so long ago yet not even a hundred hours had passed. I twisted my legs and hugged them to my chest. I pulled the comforter over my head to hold back tears.

I shuddered with dread when I remembered what December 4th meant. A memory from two years ago on that day traveled through my head and stayed like a nightmare. I was sixteen years old and had just finished grade twelve when a marriage proposal was made to me by a man who lived in Germany. Mom and Dad knew that he was an educated man from a respected family. They did not force me nor did they stop it from happening, and so we got engaged.

Our parents celebrated the cultural tradition of engagement ceremonies. I was just a follower, tagging along with the others.

The groom's family would purchase new outfits for the bride and the bride's family for the engagement party—the party boasting an exhibition of gifts and sweet baskets, along with other traditions.

Mom and Dad set a date for the engagement party, and then it was time to go shopping. The dress I chose for the party was Victorian style, inspired by the book *Rebecca*. I picked a royal blue velvet fabric with white lace around the collar and cuffs, and left it in the dressmaker's care.

The engagement party was held in our living room. Guests filled the room. I wore my hair down with a white veil flowing down my back. The music on the radio cassette player sang the traditional song, *Ahesta boro*[1] or stroll, as I walked by my father's side to the front of the room. The glow of pride from both families was apparent.

---

1   A traditional song read at Afghan weddings

For me it was like a fictitious story, a scene in a heroine's novel. Dressed in my blue velvet gown, I walked around the ballroom. But inside my grown-up body, I was still a young girl who sat in a garden of poetry, dressed all up in white, hair hanging down my shoulders, enthralled with reading and writing with my two best friends. Life for that young girl was itself a symphony of poetry.

When the night fell, I felt just like Hejazi, a Persian author. I wanted to kiss the moon and place it on to the throne of the horizon. During the day, I'd avoid talking to sailors' wives just like Bilitis from *The Songs of Bilitis*. I'd sit in the shadow of trees, waiting for my poetry teacher, Mr. Ayena, to mark the poem *Phoenix* I'd just written. I'd live in the middle of Fereydoon Moshiri's[2] alley, next to Lamartine's Lake, surrounded by Victor Hugo Saadi's flowers.

◆ ◆

ON DECEMBER 4TH, a departing ticket for Czechoslovakia and France was tucked inside my purse.

The groom's family helped me acquire a passport and visa to Paris and Germany. Getting these was a challenging process in war-torn Afghanistan, one that often involved bribery and connections with people in power in government posts.

My eyes still lingered on the stars. Sleep was too far off to even come near me. I was rigid with fear of the unknown, an icy cold wracked my body. Dawn boldly wakened me to the realization of flying, and I got up. I did not see Father at the breakfast table

---

2 Iranian poet

but I spotted him on the lower terrace of the house, pacing with unpredictability, resentment, and rage but I could tell he did not want to show it. My leaving crushed my father; it was the second time one of his children had left the Motherland. I could tell he would burst into tears any minute, but he kept it together. My father always said, "Men do not cry."

I ran to him and threw myself into his arms. I was not a man, nor did I have the strength to pretend I was. Instead, I howled.

"The taxi is waiting outside," said Gulali (the lady who helped Mom with house chores and was like a member of the family). She let out a loud cry.

I turned and kissed Grandma's hands and put my arms around her. "Bebe Kalan," I said, it was my nickname for her, "I love you."

Gulali and I hugged and kissed. I saluted the street, the house, and the neighborhood where I was raised with my teary gaze. Then, I forced myself into the taxi escorted by my mom, my youngest brother Siawash, and Shakila, my fiancé's sister.

At the Kabul airport, I made a scene because I held Mom so tightly. I did not want to leave and cried non-stop. I disregarded the direction I'd received about airport security from my parents weeks before departure.

"Parastu Jaan[3]," Dad said, using his term of endearment for me, "Just remember that leaving the country is a mystery and should remain a hidden secret. No one should know about it except immediate family members." Dad continued, "At the airport, police officers spy on passengers for signs of fleeing the country.

---

3   *Jaan* is a slang word that means *life* or *dearest*, used out of love and respect

If travelers are suspected for any reason, they are interrogated. Their flight can be cancelled and they'll receive a severe punishment from the authorities. Showing too much emotion, having too many family members at the time of departure, or unnecessary talking with customs officers will raise a red flag."

✦✦

"PARASTU, ARE YOU UP?" I heard Arash asking. My thoughts shifted. I quickly covered my mouth with my palm to hold back a cry and said nothing.

✦✦

I WANDERED BACK TO December 4th. I let go of my mom's arm and walked alone to the gate before entering the security screening area. I turned around to look at them one last time. Unspoken heartbreak warred with logic, and I swung around and ran to Mom.

"Bebe Jaan. Bebe Jaan. I—I," I said to my mom. I turned to my brother. "Siawash I—" I squeezed them tight and tried to articulate but couldn't. Sadness muted me.

"Parastu Jaan, my daughter, stay strong, you're going to be late for your flight. Go my beautiful daughter," Mom uttered as she embraced me and whispered in my ear, "Parastu Jaan, guards are watching."

In the plane, I sat in an aisle seat beside a middle-aged Afghani couple. We did not converse except for a simple *Salaam*[4], or hellos. To my right, an Afghani girl in her late twenties occupied a seat in the middle section. I looked at her and gave an amicable smile. She smiled back.

"Salam sister, I am Parastu," I said.

"I am Najiba, Salaam," she replied. I saw tears roll down her cheeks as she wiped them with the back of her hand. I reached out to pat her arm but said nothing.

I leaned my head back and closed my eyes, shedding my own tears as the aircraft soared from the ground. Hours later, as the aircraft passed through beds of clouds, a deep voice echoed through the plane.

"We are crossing the last air space of Afghanistan," the pilot announced.

In that moment, the entire plane transformed as everyone wept. The passengers' sorrow revealed the pain of fleeing their homeland.

After almost seven hours of flying, the plane landed at the Prague airport late afternoon. Najiba and I followed everyone to the baggage claim area. She got her suitcases, but mine was not there.

"Najiba Jaan," I said, "You can go. I'll meet you at customs." The baggage claim area grew empty. I panicked and ran to the information desk.

---

4   *Salaam* is *hello* in Farsi Dari

"Hello," I pushed my passport and ticket under the kiosk slot. I continued, "I can't find my suitcase." The lady on the other side punched in some numbers from my passport.

"Your bags are on their way to Paris." She pushed my papers back through the slot.

I headed to the customs and border area, moving fast to catch up with Najiba. I pushed my way through passengers and arrived, breathing heavily, at the end of a long line-up. I spotted Najiba standing in the middle of the line as she waved.

After a long wait, I approached the customs officer, who sat comfortably behind a desk with a protective glass window.

"Hello sir," I said with a raspy voice and showed him my passport and ticket. The officer gazed at me and said something in his language that I didn't understand, but his tone sounded doubtful.

He returned my documents and expressed in English, "Miss, no visa, you cannot enter the country."

I couldn't believe what I'd just heard. The flow of oxygen stopped moving through my bloodstream, every part of me still. The officer pushed the passport underneath the glass window as his image blurred before my eyes. He continued, "You have two options. One, in about four hours, a plane leaves for Kabul. Two, to get a twenty-four hour transit visa to stay here until your next flight."

I took my passport and stumbled backward like an erratic wind towards the end of the line-up. The officer's voice seemed to echo all around me.

Kabul. Kabul. Kabul. Visa. Visa. Visa.

My legs lost the ability to walk any further. I approached a wall beside customs and bent down on the floor. I hid my face between my knees and sobbed. A male voice only deepened my humiliation, and I raised my head. The couple who'd sat beside me on the plane shook their heads as they passed by and said in Farsi-Dari, "You ruin the Afghan's reputation with your non-stop tears."

Najiba got her luggage and was ready to leave the airport, yet she came to check on me. A gentle touch on my shoulder inter-rupted my despondence.

"What is going on Parastu, are you okay?" Her soothing voice reminded me of the conversation I'd had with Mom and Dad two days before the flight.

"Parastu, when you arrive at the Prague airport, you will be attended by a woman named Khaleda. Khaleda Jaan is Uncle Shams's sister. She lives in Prague and works at the Afghan Embassy." Dad continued, "Uncle Shams has informed his sister of your arrival time. She will pick you up at the airport and take you to her home overnight and then she will take you back to the airport the next day."

I stood up and explained the dilemma to Najiba and asked her, "Please go out to the arrival area and look for someone holding a sign with my name on it. Her name is Khaleda, she works for the Afghan Embassy. Explain my circumstances and see if she can get me a transit visa. She's my only hope, or I have to go back home."

"Parastu, do not worry and do not even think of going back home. You don't know what the Kabul police would do to you. I promise you, we will find a way." Her strength and support gave me the peace I needed to calm down.

"Thank you so much, Najiba Jaan," I said as my voice quivered, and then we parted.

At around midnight, the three of us left the airport holding Najiba's arms, listening to Khaleda as we boarded a transit bus for her apartment.

◆◆

THE SUNRISE OF DECEMBER 5th came like the warm caress of a mother's touch, but left me cold as a twist of grey fog reminded me of my final destination. Air France flew me to Paris airport.

Sheck sheck—the sound of an inked block brought down on the document. The customs officer stamped my passport.

"Welcome to Paris," he said.

Paris, the city of literature and the arts. As we called it back home, Paris is the bride compared to the other cities of the world. I'd visited this gem of a city many times through novels and po-etry with Victor Hugo, Alexandre Dumas, Voltaire, Honoré de Balzac, and Alphonse de Lamartine. How often I fancied a walk along the famous Avenue des Champs-Élysées of Paris, drinking tea at a coffee shop near the Eiffel Tower.

The sliding door opened, and I saw my fiancé waiting in the crowd. I hesitated, a faint emotion weighed upon me, and I let other passengers pass by. Gradually, I wandered out, pulled myself together, and waved. After months, days, and hours of a long-distance, arranged engagement, I finally confronted the face of my future. And I felt empty.

Chapter Two

I lifted my head from under the quilt and gasped for air. The digital alarm clock on the nightstand read 7:30 in the morning. A bursting sound flew around the room as Arash breathed. I hadn't seen Arash in five years. My parents had sent him away to avoid being recruited into the military.

..

I WAS ON the cusp of adolescence and adulthood when the proxy war between Mujahedeen and the Afghan government (Khalq and Parcham) started. In December 1979, as snow fell from a gray sky on Kabul's heart, the release of Russian tanks on the street braced the spirit of Afghans for a cruel winter. The Communist government was in power. It was a state of political corruption and a condition of extreme panic and anxiety. Afghanistan faced massive evil and segregation.

Father inked his concern on paper by writing about the corrupt history of our land and hiding it in the attic. Houses were inspected by government officials for suspicious material or signs of any conspiracy against the government.

My father gathered us once and said, "At school, do not mention that you are Tajik," an ethnic group which spoke Farsi-Dari, "Also remember not to say anything against the current state of the government."

It was rumored the government had spies everywhere, and any wrongdoing or speaking against the government would get you incarcerated. A proverb circulated among people during the dictatorship and terror. *The walls have mice and mice have ears.* It was a campaign of genocide.

Military recruitment was compulsory, done by force, with young boys collected from the streets and sent into the armed forces. Arash, when he was thirteen and running late for school, left home in a hurry. It wasn't until late in the afternoon when Arash was not home yet that Mom started panicking. *Where was Arash?* She ran to his room, to ensure he had his ID card and found it laying on his desk.

All young boys were required to carry an ID card with them. Armed guards patrolled the city and asked young boys for ID cards. If they could not prove their age, they were pulled into the Army. It was also said that young boys were asked to pull up their pant legs for hair growth inspection for military judgement.

Mom's piercing cry signaled danger and with a lightning speed, she ran to the family room.

"Arash, Arash forgot to take his ID!" She breathed harshly. With a red face and wide eyes, Dad stood up from the mattress[5] where he'd been relaxing. School had ended for the day, and they had no idea where he was nor where to go for help. Dad quickly dressed

---

5   Afghanistan family rooms were furnished with a mattress and matching pillows

and left the house to search for him while Mom called around. Siawash was eight years old at the time, and I was three years older than him. Siawash and I stood close by the phone, holding hands while we sobbed quietly.

Twilight conquered the horizon. The silence in the house, along with the evening shadows, revealed a troubling scene, making us break out in a cold sweat. Dad was gone for nearly two hours. We did not want to imagine what might happen next. Inevitably, we fixated on the horrible possibility that Arash and Dad had gone missing. Dusk's vagueness condensed as fear clung to us.

Three hours after Dad's departure the front yard door opened and Dad and Arash entered.

"After school, I headed home," Arash said. He said nothing after that.

Mom made him juice and said, "It is fine now. You are safe."

He lay down, the blood rushing to his ears. His hands were cold. Mom and Dad gazed at one another with strained eyes. Mom pressed her index finger to her lips as her gaze flitted to us. Siawash and I sat by his side, our heads hung low. After a couple of still hours, Arash tried to explain his forgotten ID card that morning.

"On my way to the bus stop, I was stopped by a soldier and asked for ID. I reached into my pocket, and it was empty. They pulled me on to a military transport. I was the youngest man on the vehicle," he said. "The sun was falling in the west. I thought that was it. I was doomed. My legs were like icicles. I was chewing on my nails when I noticed that the soldier who was in charge of the military vehicle was standing alone beside the car. He turned his face and shot a direct gaze at me. He gestured for me to get down from the car. My heart leaped to my mouth. I was scared to move but I forced my body down the truck. The soldier brought his head closer and whispered, 'Bacha Jaan[6], when I turn my face to the opposite side, you run home. Never leave your house without your ID.'"

THE DANGER OF WAR forced individuals to flee for security. Families escaped to Pakistan, Iran, and India via planes, cars, and on foot or animals. The second step was to get to one of the western countries for a landed immigrant status from Pakistan or India.

One day my father's friend came to visit him as I was serving them tea. I heard my dad's friend howling and pleading with tears running into his white beard to my father to save Arash's life. The man had lost his own son to the Army, and he never came home. My father's friend was an incredibly proud man and would never allow himself to be seen with tears in his eyes. Yet, this moment brought out his emotion in a way that I've never seen before. His tears revealed the gravity of circumstances to Father, which ultimately convinced him to send Arash abroad. My patriot father dreamed of a peaceful and united country and his children's return, which was the only reason he did not want to leave the country.

---

6   Bacha Jaan is a slang word for boy

My dad was almost six feet in height, an average build with gray hair. But there was something about the way he dressed, he always looked dapper. His socks matched his shirt and suit and he always stated, "Fashion comes from England." Karakul hats with different shades were popular among Afghanistan men, and Father coordinated the hat with the suit he put on. White was his favorited color.

My grandfather, Mirza Mohammad Mehdi Chindawoly, was King Amanullah Khan's head secretary (sar monshi) and a member of the constitutional party (Jamiat mashrota khahy). Nader Khan executed him while the King was exiled. After the execution, the government banned my father and his two brothers from school and working at government companies. My father was in fourth grade.

My grandmother Bobo Jaan, at the age of twenty-five years, was widowed with five children and no income. Yet, she wanted her sons to be educated like their father.

My father and his two brothers studied at home and were taught by the elders of the community. When my father grew older, some of my grandfather's friends took him under their wings and gave him an entry-level position at the Nasaji Afghan, a fabric company. After that, Father started taking night classes studying accounting while working during the day. He slowly moved his way up the company with his hard work and dedication, later becoming its CEO. Father was also a parliament member at the age of forty and a member of the constitutional party with a platform declaring democracy and human rights.

Once Father, along with some of their party members, met with King Zahir Shah and as young democrats, they pleaded, "Please grant the people only the rights of a British laborer."

Yet, while Daoud Khan was prime minister, the government conspired against Dad and his party. My father, along with a few of his party members, were imprisoned for six years without trial even though they had not committed any crime.

Father was always saying, "Where there is no law, living is impossible."

My father, at a very young age, started reading books. He told the story, "My mother one day asked me to get her something from the *gow sandoq*, or the strongbox. When I opened the box, my eyes got caught on one of my dad's books called *Hidden Island*. I brought it along with me and started reading. That was the turning point."

I have never seen anyone love books like my father. If Mom did not call him for a meal, he wouldn't even notice the passing of time while he read. My father was a historian. He was busy writing the history of Afghanistan titled, *Notes and Impressions from the Durrani Empire*. My mother and I were doing the proofreading.

⁓⁓

AT NINETEEN YEARS OLD, Arash was more of a man, no longer the boy that I remembered. He'd grown much taller than me. His dark brown hair reminded me of Elvis's famous sideburns. When we reunited after years of distance, I cried. Father's hope for his son's return was shattered, yet he'd sent another child overseas.

Arash lived with our cousin, a war survivor who'd fled home at the age of fourteen. The sky, the ground, the climate, and the time were completely different from where I was born.

I closed my eyes, hoping for it all to be a bad dream, to wake up in my own room in Karte Parwan. I envisioned Mom's voice resonating, calling my name, "Parastu Jaan, breakfast is ready. Are you up?" Arash, Siawash, Dad, Mom, Grandma Bebe Kalan, and I would go to the family room, and Dad would sing a song and joke to make us all laugh.

I surrendered to the truth that I'd left my home and family for good.

Would I ever be able to see them again?

It was a question that I could not answer at that moment. Only destiny could answer it for me. I got up from the bed, saw Arash opening his eyes, greeted him, and went to the bathroom to wash.

Everything was different. Back home, we lived in a house with big rooms, bathrooms, and a kitchen.

I opened the bathroom door. It was small, but one huge difference was the warm water. Back home, we had a boiler installed on the wall near the sink. Mother turned it on to get warm water before waking up in the morning, which was only available if we had power. Otherwise, a Solo Stove Titan was used to boil water. For the shower, we had a wood burner water heater in each bathroom. In winter, we had wood-burning stoves to warm up a room, but only in one or two main rooms. So the entire house, except for the family room, was always cold.

I thought to myself that a warm bath would help eliminate the nervous exhaustion. So, I entered the bathtub, closed the shower curtain, and nourished my wounded being with warm water while I wept slowly. Then, we got ready to go to my Aunt Razia's house for breakfast.

My aunt's apartment was considered far away. I recalled that last night my cousin drove us back from my aunt's apartment. Auntie had invited everyone for dinner to celebrate my arrival and then invited Arash and I back for breakfast the next morning.

Aunt Razia, Uncle Gul[7] (a nickname we picked out of respect for auntie's husband), and their three children had fled Afghanistan seven years earlier to escape the war.

We had to take a twenty-minute bus ride to the central bus station at Viersen, followed by a fifteen-minute walk. Arash had the exact change when we entered the bus and dropped the money into the fare machine. Everything was strange to me, and I compared it with home. The fare for the buses back home was collected by a male collector. Once the bus started driving, the collector passed through and collected money for the bus at each bus stop and granted the ticket.

We got off at the station and started walking, crossing the main street or *Hauptstraße*. The Hauptstraße lined with clothing stores and restaurants was the city's center. The bazaar, as we say it in Farsi-Dari, was packed. I was stunned by how many businesses there were on both sides of the road. Arash was explaining the various shops, their business hours, and some of the German terms. The German language sounded heavy and abstruse compared to both my native tongue and English. English was taught as a second language in school, but the phrases Arash used felt like whole sentences for only one word.

---

7   *Gul* means *flower*

We were just about to make a left turn when a clothing store caught my attention. I was transfixed by the clothes displayed in the window. I'd always loved clothes and dressing up—I still do. Back home, I picked up new styles from European catalogues. Mom and I requested them at the tailor shop, and we provided the fabric.

A childhood memory played before my eyes. On a Friday afternoon, Mom planned a trip to the tailor shop and dragged Siawash and me along. Any time Mom took us to the city center she treated us to a restaurant or ice cream. Siawash was five years old, and we were inseparable.

She had dropped off the fabric for a dress the week before. The shop was big, with several tailors working. We entered and greeted the head tailor. Men held all of these jobs. The head tailor gave Mom her dress to try on and she headed to the fitting room, an area with curtains for privacy.

Siawash and I stared at the sewing machines in the middle of the store as the sound of the electric rhythm clunked, ground, and stormed all around us. Our focus shifted from one device to the next. We were enamored by the sight of all those appliances. Finally, a young tailor who was about fifteen years old noticed our perplexed gazes and asked Siawash if he wanted to try the sewing machine. Siawash looked at me and eagerly joined the boy on the opposite side of his desk to better understand those noisy tools.

Siawash dropped to the ground as the machine flew over his head, not even a couple of minutes into his zealous sewing. Siawash's upper lip was cut by the machine's needle before it landed beside him. The entire store stopped breathing at once, and a stillness emerged. Siawash was covered in blood. The three of us ended up at the hospital in horror.

"Do you want to go inside the clothing store?" Arash asked. I quickly returned to the present.

"No, it's fine. I can look from here," I answered. I looked back at the store and noticed a woman of about forty dressing the mannequin. As we passed, my eyes caught the salesclerk's, and she smiled a silent greeting.

Across the shop was a small, fast-food restaurant called *Imbiss* in the German language. Arash explained that they sell hamburgers, sausages, and French fries.

I've always loved French fries. As a child, I was a picky eater and never ate much. I certainly didn't eat every meal that was prepared. Most of the time, I pretended I wasn't hungry, but Mom knew. So she would make me French fries. She would ask me to peel potatoes and cut them into small pieces, and then she would take over and fry them for me, serving them with home-made ketchup.

I also loved to bring stories home from school and tell them to Mom and the rest of the family. She would listen to me for hours while she did her housework and I chased her around.

Dad would always say, "My daughter goes two blocks down the street and surprises us with two pages of stories. Imagine if she goes on a long journey!"

Like my father, I have been a lover of books and writing since my teenage years. I shared my thoughts on poetry and books with Dad. The first two books that introduced me to literature were given to me by my father. I was an eleven-year-old, timid preteen presented with *Jenayati Bashar* or *Human Crimes*, and

Bakhoda Man Fahisha Nistam or *God, I am not a Prostitute.* Those two books introduced me to society and, as a teenage girl, were an eye-opener into our male-dominated country.

Mom was a chemistry professor at the Pharmacy faculty. She was average in height and size and has always had short hair. Every morning she would put rollers in her hair, whether she was working or not. She used to squeeze a fresh lemon and massage her scalp before using the rollers. She never used hair products or nail polish. Eyeliner and a light brown lipstick were her only make-up. Her serious persona intimidated most male teenagers who lived in our neighborhood. If she caught a young boy in our street smoking, Mom would walk towards them, grab their cigarette, throw it on the ground, and step on it. Then she lectured them. And they would not utter a word to defend themselves; they would just bow their heads.

I recalled these things as I walked with Arash. He told stories about school, life, and his time apart from us. I was listening, but the pain of goodbyes still lingered in my thoughts and heart.

As we walked, I noticed lots of apartments but not many houses. Nobody troubled anybody. It did not matter if you were a woman or a man; everybody was busy with their own thoughts. This was not the case back home. Women were often discriminated against. It was a common occurrence for women to be victims of harassment daily.

No familiar faces to stop and say hello and Arash murmured in my ear that we had arrived at my aunt's building.

The building my Aunt Razia lived in was taller than my brother's three-story building. We arrived on the fourth floor, and Arash rang the bell to her apartment.

Tarana, my cousin, opened the door, and we greeted each other with three kisses, one on each cheek. Aunt Razia was known for her cooking. She prepared the special Afghani tea called *Shir chia,* a kind of milk tea, and all kinds of home-baked cookies. It was a complete meal, but I had no appetite for food and did not eat much. We talked about the people we had left behind and also about my future.

The memory of last night played before my eyes. My fiancé and I had arrived late in the afternoon from Paris. He'd stayed for dinner and then left late at night to go home. All my cousins were there and after dinner, they performed live music in honor of my arrival. Arash and my cousins played the Armonia[8] and the Tabla[9] while they sang. My fiancé sat around them. They staged the entertainment on a Persian rug. It is a common courtesy to artists to match their position by sitting on the ground. I sat on the couch beside Auntie across the music venue as my eyes teared up.

My fiancé tried to catch my gaze from time to time, but my eyes were everywhere except on him. I set my eyes on the music and wondered how strange it was that I could not even look at him.

He also attempted to start a conversation by getting closer and asked, "Are you fine? Do you need anything?"

"I'm fine. Thanks," I answered quickly, staring at the hand that stabbed my thigh. It felt like I was caught in a desert storm. All I wanted was to curl up and sleep to get away.

---

8   Keyboard instrument

9   Drum instrument

"Parastu Jaan, we should head home. It's getting late and I have to go to school tomorrow," Arash said. Arash had missed school to be with me today. Three kisses for goodbyes and then we left. Evening descended on the town and the cold chills that struck my body made me long for a heated home. We slowly made our way back to my brother's apartment. As we approached the clothing store that caught my eyes earlier, I turned to look at the store and again saw the sales lady inside. She nodded her head in greeting and smiled at me. I smiled back, then quickly turned and kept walking.

✦✦

IN THE TWO MONTHS since my arrival to Germany I made every attempt to accept the fact of this relationship and that I would get married. My fiancé and I met several times on the weekends. Any time we were together, there was a silence in my soul. The idea that we were engaged nurtured strong feeling of hostility in me.

Then, one Sunday afternoon when my fiancé came to visit, a thunderstorm jolted my emptiness. Rain poured on the heart of February. I imagined how the sky opened its inner self to the Earth and washed away the dirt on its surface. He was driving, the car roof an umbrella over my head. The rattling sound of raindrops intensified my inner cry.

"Stop the car. Please, stop the car!" I yelled.

He parked the car in the nearest parking lot. He noticed my avoidance but did not know what to do.

"Are you okay?" he asked.

"No, I'm not okay. You are a fine young man and I am so sorry. . ."

I could not continue, and my tears fell like the rain outside. Finally, I gathered myself.

"I cannot proceed with this relationship. I tried. I tried. You deserve better but I am not ready."

He looked out the front window. Silence filled the car. The sound of rain beating on top of the vehicle penetrated this stillness and blew harder. He looked back to me then broke the silence with his heavy breathing.

"I support your decision," he said, "There's no need for us to continue. We will let others know. I'll let my family know and you do the same thing. I know it will be hard on them, but I respect your wish."

Our break-up was not easy to swallow for our families. The cultural burden of what others would think troubled them. Fundamentally, our surroundings dictate our biographies. In our society, we live for others. They relied on the integrity of arranged marriages to succeed. Both families were left disappointed. My parents respected my decision, yet they were confused about what I would do after the failed engagement.

I looked in the mirror and saw myself as a free young woman with the vision to go to university and be somebody. I wanted to experience the flow of spring and summer and winter as I grew among them, to develop the little girl inside me living in the garden of poetry. I touched my collarbone with a trembling hand and asked, *how would I look tomorrow?* I held my own hand and walked on the path of life in this strange new land.

Chapter Three

I kept going to my auntie's house regularly. Taking the bus became very easy for me. Every day, except Sundays, between 10 a.m. and 11 a.m., the postman delivered our mail. This was my lifeline home, and it felt like something substantial to begin my day with a letter from my parents. In the morning, before leaving the apartment, I would run downstairs in hopes of a letter from home. I never wanted to step out before eleven. Existence continued its regular spinning as it rotated my destiny and the destinies of billions of people around the world.

The season of awakening was upon us. It was not waiting for a perfect day to arrive it simply surprised us with its rebirth. One day the doorbell rang around three in the afternoon and I wondered who it could be. Arash was home from school. I peeked from the kitchen window and saw the mail man. I rushed downstairs in barefoot.

"Hello sir," I said.

"I have a telegram for you," he replied, handing it to me.

"Siawash is in Czechoslovakia, help him," it read. Mom had sent it from Kabul.

"Arash, Arash! Look, Mom sent this message, what should we do?" I entered Arash's room and disturbed his studies.

"Call Uncle Gul and Auntie and let them know," Arash said.

I quickly dialed their number. They said to come over to discuss it further since they'd received the same telegram.

Arash and I held our racing hearts tight as we caught the bus going to the Central Station. With trembling knees we arrived at their apartment like two ghosts in the daylight and exchanged the three kisses in greeting. We had no knowledge of what had happened to Siawash, Mom, Dad, and Grandma Bebe Kalan. All four of us, Uncle, Aunt, Arash, and I sat around the dining table in their hallway, waiting to receive a phone call either from Siawash in Czechoslovakia or a call from Kabul, Afghanistan, to speak to my parents.

Life in Afghanistan had revolved around the horrendous war, which savagely dominated Kabul, the capital city. Bomb explosions, bloodshed, and killing sprees were a daily occurrence. The country was hungry for youngsters' blood to join the war. The military recruitment of half-grown boys was getting out of control. Teenagers hid at home to escape death. War tried to make living miserable for civilians. Even inside, homes were unsafe as the military interrogated people.

Darkness, the thief of bold spirit, hovered above us like a night owl. Silence was interrupted only by our hammering heartbeats.

Jerrrrr! The phone's ringing moved us from our seats as we all faced Uncle at once. After the second ring, he picked up the phone without hesitation.

"Hello?" Uncle yelled. He quickly turned the speakerphone on.

"Uncle Gul, salaam. It's Siawash." His tormented voice sounded desperate as he continued. "I arrived in Czechoslovakia with Dad's friend this afternoon. Dad's friend is a business man who was supposed to stay here for couple months, but he received a message from Kabul that he had to return immediately. He leaves tomorrow. I am in this hotel until he leaves. What should I do? Where should I go?" His voice sank into despair.

Uncle remained calm. "Do not worry. We will help you stay at the hotel. We will call you back soon. Do you have money?"

"Yes, yes, yes," Siawash said.

"Please don't go anywhere," my uncle emphasized and asked for the hotel's address.

Siawash started spelling the name in English. "C," he stuttered.

But Uncle was used to the German alphabet and asked, "Siawash, what is C? Do you mean Sah?"

"No, C," said Siawash.

An annoyed Uncle asked, "Do you mean C in Farsi-Dari?" C is number thirty in numerical terms.

Siawash gave up. "Uncle Gul, please draw a semicircle."

Arash and I smiled at each other despite the frustration.

Arash and Uncle brainstormed all the possibilities while Arash began pacing around the table. Uncle covered his face with his palms. Arash's steps grew heavier, terror arresting his heart.

Horror tortured my hope and twisted my gut. Siawash, an orphan child of combat, found himself miles from home in a strange hotel room. I could picture him with his head held between his knees, waiting on a phone call to determine his future.

I got mad and cried out in dread, "What if he can't make it through the night? Oh God please, please help my baby brother. I am going to die if anything bad happens to Siawash."

Auntie hugged me and I lowered my head on her shoulder and cried.

Arash finally spoke, "I have a friend whose father works for the government. This is all I've got." His voice thickened as he continued, "It's seven in the evening and a work night, but hopefully they won't mind answering the phone."

Arash dialed the number. Luckily, Arash's friend picked up the phone, and after greeting, Arash, in complete disaster, explained Siawash's condition. Arash's friend said he would talk to his dad and call back.

Before hanging up the phone he asked, "How old is your brother?"

"Fourteen," Arash said.

I could sense every second of every minute. It was so tangible; the clock with its tick-tock thrummed with my nerves. Two hours passed and my hope succumbed, furthermore, my confidence shattered.

The phone rang and Uncle picked it up and passed it to Arash, who pressed the speaker.

"My father knows someone at the International Amnesty," Arash's friend said, "The gentleman at the Amnesty said since your brother is under the age of eighteen, he does not need a visa to cross the border."

We all looked at one other and then back to the phone.

Arash's friend continued, "Tell your brother to buy a train ticket to Germany tomorrow morning and then you can pick him up at the border. I will get back to you with the train schedule and name of the station and border," he said.

All four of us leaned back in our chairs. The phone call phenomenon was surreal; we all gazed at the phone and could not believe what had just happened. All night we were up, waiting to connect to Kabul to let my parents know Siawash was safe.

The next day Arash, Uncle, and a gentleman from International Amnesty, drove to the border. The train that carried Siawash stopped at the edge. Arash and Uncle stood, searching every passenger who got off the train. Arash had left Afghanistan when Siawash was nine years old, and they both had changed. Arash would not recognize Siawash, but Siawash would since he'd seen pictures of Arash.

Siawash was in the train cabin, paralyzed. The screaming steam whistle sound echoed through the train station. Siawash wondered if the scrutinizing eyes of each passenger sensed his alienation.

"Siawash, Siawash, Siawash. There he is." He covered his ears as the voices got closer. "Arrest him!"

He froze.

The train was almost empty, but there was no sign of Siawash. Arash raced inside the train, searching for him. Meanwhile, Siawash saw a man who resembled Arash inspecting the cabin, but he was skeptical. A visceral reaction overtook Siawash's trembling body. He walked towards the young man with black hair and their eyes met, both wondering if those eyes could be of the same childhood.

In broken English Siawash uttered, "I am sorry, Afghan? Name Arash?"

Siawash had grown taller since we'd parted four months ago. He was taller than Arash now. His black hair and eyes were that of a handsome young man. Arash, and now Siawash, lessened the pain of separation for me.

A telegram was sent to my parents in Kabul with the story of us three reunified. The waiting period my parents endured for news of their son was like a month of Sundays.

◆ ◆

SUMMER CAME AND WENT. The days were getting shorter as the naked trees shivered in the cold. Three seasons had passed since I'd arrived in Germany. I had to face the consequences of my engagement break-up first. It was an ugly separation. Even though everything ended with a mutual understanding, Afghans and relatives who knew my fiancé were in denial and had no mercy. They shunned me from social gatherings if my fiancé was present. My immigration application was denied. Now I was only a refugee. My status was filled with blank pages, like an inkless printer.

On the morning of October 18th, I left the apartment after the postman had delivered a few flyers, to catch the bus for Hauptstraße. It was my nineteenth birthday and I wanted to get a cake and a candle to celebrate with Siawash in the evening. Siawash had registered for Realschule, or secondary school, the following month of his arrival to Germany and began his grade nine studies. Arash and my cousin had both left for university in a different city after summer.

I walked along the main street. I was getting familiar with the city center. I even learned where it starts and finishes. The shops on both sides made the city even more attractive. Crowds had come and gone. The smiles and energy of youngsters, the elders' curiosity, and the childrens' absurdity and playfulness added extra charm to the central city. There was so much to entice me yet all these distractions only added noise to my unknown tomorrow. Inside I was screaming for help. I thought of my dream, to go to university and be somebody, but I didn't know how or where to begin.

As I paraded through the street, I wondered why after I started adolescence, my life pulled in so many different directions?

⁌ ⁌

AFTER WINTER BREAK OF 1984, I transitioned to Zargona High School and made friends with a few girls in our class. One girl with whom I became best friends with was Kahkashan. Kahkashan's big, brown eyes glowed beside her olive skin reminiscent of the beauty of an Indian movie star. She scored top grades in the class. We both were in love with poetry and literature. We wrote prose poetry and shared them with one another. We always exchanged books and talked about literature but silently chose to study science. We never discussed our future faculty. Medicine was practical enough. No need to discuss or think, it was an obvious choice.

In our culture, becoming a doctor or engineer was the dream of every parent, especially if someone scored good grades. Medicine was a programmed selection by default. My father always said, "Human characters and personalities evolve from three aspects of life. First: Genes and parenting. Second: Friends and social crowds. Third: Society and environment. 'Tell me first who your friends are, then I will tell you who you are.'" Father would end his spiel with the two first verses of Saadi Shirazi, the Persian poet.

In elementary and high school, we had written and oral exams to pass each class for the language Farsi-Dari. The teacher always asked me, "Parastu, if you translate the next poem of the text-book, you will be excused from the verbal exam."

Writing sentences on the board was one of our daily activities in language class at high school.

"Life is a tale, told by an idiot—Shakespeare." I wrote on the board.

"Erase it at once before I send you to the principal's office," the teacher shouted at me from behind her desk. I did not understand the teacher's outburst.

On some occasions I heard the instructor making remarks. "Parastu, I heard your prose poem broadcasted on the radio."

Or, "Parastu, I read your prose poem in a magazine. You are building a good reputation for our school." My love of literature led me to writing prose poetry. Yet, I was yelled at that what I read was wrong. Where did that leave me?

I'd fantasized about a white lab coat while my family planned my engagement. Before my entry exam for university, I sought guidance from one of my cousins who was a doctor. She suggested a few things and told me stories of her anatomy studies, practicing on dead bodies.

When I went back home, I could not sleep for several nights and begged Siawash to keep the lights on at night. Siawash and I shared a bedroom, but when Arash left I got his room and turned it into my own realm of poetry. I put the desk in the middle of the room facing the window that overlooked the front yard. On the walls I hung poems and romantic pictures I cut from the magazines.

I signed up for an afterschool math class. I worked with classmates on mock exams and spent sleepless nights reviewing science and math for the entry exam.

The night before the exam, when twilight fluttered against the blue sky, I finished my closing study of the summary I'd prepared. I completed my tasks and announced my readiness. The next day I woke early, covered in sweat. My heart knocked on the walls of my chest, roaring to get out. I fiddled with the plate at the breakfast table. I did not want to eat, but Mom advised eating for strength. I kissed everyone goodbye, and Grandma Bebe Kalan prayed Ayat Al-Kursi and blew a chof-chof[10], or a sound, on my face in the spirit of God. Mom and Dad gave me moral support.

The exam was at the University of Kabul in the Faculty of Science. I took the bus and arrived at the meeting point arranged by my classmates. After the exam, I met with friends outside. I felt exhausted and satisfied. I realized the exam was not as challenging as I expected. We were informed the results would be sent to the school within a month.

On the announcement day, my mother accompanied me to school. She knew how important that day was for me. The bus

---

10   Traditional prayer sound, blown onto the face

stopped across from school and we got off and walked to the door. A *chaprassy*[11], or the female school crew, searched our bodies and purses, and then we went to the building.

I greeted familiar faces but did not see any of my friends since we had not arranged a meetup. I noticed in the corridor a vast circle of students gathered near a glass display case on the wall, filled with papers. I looked at Mom and ran towards the crowd. I pushed my way to the board and searched for my family name.

Ahang, Parastu—Faculty of Geology, the document read.

I rushed back to where Mom was standing, in complete denial. I asked her to investigate, to check if what I'd seen was correct. I saw Mom pacing slowly back, pressing her lips together. A dark cloud covered my eyes, and the concrete floor beneath my feet swayed. I stumbled and passed out in Mom's arms.

I grieved. I didn't know a faculty by the name of Geology even existed. I didn't know what it even meant. I protested. Dad wrote a letter addressed to the Minister of Education. Mom booked an appointment with the University Chancellor. Mom and I, along with the letter, met with the Chancellor. Mom asked that we wanted to dispute and presented the letter. Dad pointed out the illicit systemic problems maneuvered in the government. The Chancellor laid out a few plans to arbitrate the dispute.

"I am sorry," he said, "I cannot review this since the academic year has already started. However, I can offer her a few options." His gaze landed on me and he continued, "First, I can award her a scholarship to any allied countries overseas to advance to Medical." Mom and I were all ears. "Second, she can work at the

---

11   Security

university for this year and next then I will enroll her into the Faculty of Medicine." We got up in disappointment, declined all those options, and left.

Mom was telling us stories of a distressing experience she'd had with her male students.

"Male students who failed class were forced into the Army," she explained, "While students who were part of the government party, or had support from a mediator, unfairly received passing grades."

A few days after mourning for my future, I woke up with a high-strung body aches on my arms, back and legs. With the advice of a doctor, Mom administered vials of Vitamin B1, 6, and 12 shots. My body went to a complete shock, with rashes covering my body, including my head and face.

In 1987, the new school year began, and I enrolled in the Kabul University Faculty of Geology majoring in meteorology.

♦ ♦

"WATCH WHERE YOU'RE GOING!" a female voice screamed in my ear as I was about to step on her toe.

"I am so sorry, ma'am," I said and turned around to go to the bakery in the opposite direction.

The sun followed a lower path in the blue sky and the days had been trimmed of their sharp edges. The year's end was approaching in thirty days, and it was time to form a new resolution.

I heard the key turn in the locked door and a set of lucid eyes with a subtle smile entered.

"Salaam Hamshira Jaan," said Siawash. This is a slang word for sister. Without hesitation, he continued, "Frau[12] Bors, my language teacher wants to meet with you. She wants to teach you the language," he said.

I stood up at once, my spirit dancing. I hugged him tightly and squealed, "Wahoo! Is this real?" Siawash brought an early spring to the winter of my soul's condition.

When I'd left home, I could only bring two books and my poetry notebook. I'd left my diaries in a friend's hands since they were cumbersome and I did not want to raise any red flags at the airport. The two books were Deewan-e-Hafiz, a Persian poet, and *The Prophet* by Khalil Gibran. Reading Hafiz's poem was like an anti-depressant, particularly Fali Hafiz. It brought comfort and gave me hope that life will turn around.

"Tomorrow morning we go to school together," Siawash continued as he entered the kitchen. "She wants to meet with you before class begins, to lay out plans for your tutorial."

Christine Bors was a German language teacher at Realschule, where my brothers and cousins studied. Frau Bors knew about the war that has dominated Afghanistan for decades and she was very aware of the world crisis. I held Dewani Hafiz pressed to my chest like a little girl with an abundance of excitement. I went to bed for the first day of school and, possibly, to a new beginning.

---

12   The title for addressing a woman in the German language

Chapter Four

*R*ing. . . *ring*. . . *ring*.

My alarm clock went off as dawn slowly broke over the town. I hurried to kiss the gloom goodbye. I jumped out of bed, remembering my first day of school after winter break back home. The ironed uniform and polished footwear waited restlessly in the closet. The notebooks were purchased a week before and each ascribed a title. A pencil case with blue, black, and red pens sat inside my brown school bag. The bag waved from the desk, ready to fly on my shoulder. Before leaving for school, I would ask Mom my routine question, "Are you going to be home today?" If the answer was yes, I felt at ease, prepared to come back with loads of stories.

I went to the bathroom before Siawash was up. The hot water rushed through the pipes as I turned the faucet and quickly mixed hot and cold before entering the tub. A stream of warm water danced over my head and body and doubled the feel-good vibes.

I visited the kitchen and tried to feed my empty stomach, but only a glass of water served me well. The daylight knocked at the window, and I raced back to the bedroom. I dressed in sky-blue jeans with a long-sleeved turndown collar; a button-up red and black sweater covered my slim figure. The outfits I'd brought from home were all packed back in the suitcase and left on top of the closet. The bag held semi-formal attire: skirts and dresses and high heels. I checked the fashion trends for young adults and followed those. Brand names weren't my objective. I didn't know about them nor did I have the money. I left my hair with a deep side parting and applied face cream, lipstick, and perfume.

Siawash and I took the bus to school. The bus stop was across from our apartment, and we got in and sat down. The bus stopped at several stations, and with each stop, I looked at Siawash to see if it was ours.

At the next stop my gaze fixed on Siawash's calm and happy face and I thought about how attached I was to this young man. If we ever argued over something, and he was to leave the apartment, I would grab and hold him tight in my arms. The abrupt threat of parting would scare me, and I would run to him. Our next-door neighbor mentioned that she enjoyed it when she heard us laughing.

Taking pictures of passing seasons was my favorite hobby, and Siawash and I bought a small, affordable camera. One afternoon in mid-summer, as the golden rays of sun inspired our inner artists, Siawash said, "Hamshira Jaan, let's go out by the pond to take pictures."

Near the apartment was a narrow body of water in the middle of a small forest surrounded by tall trees. I put on jeans with a pink blouse and left my long hair down, crowning my head with a pink and gold Indian scarf. I modeled in front of the camera. He shot numerous poses. By the end of the day, he declared that the camera had actually had only one photo left on the roll of film. The sound of our laughter reached the sky and to the other side of the ocean, to our parents.

The school building appeared in the distance, a two-story structure with a small front yard where boys and girls mingled freely. All the students were the same age as Siawash or younger, and I did not see many foreigners. He went ahead and waved at his classmates as he passed by the front yard, and I followed him. We entered the hallway where the principal stood, greeting students and ensuring everyone went to their classes. We moved forward, and my brother introduced me to him.

He acknowledged us with a smile. The second bell rang at that moment and I saw a woman almost one inch shorter than me with short golden hair walking in our direction. She had a black skirt and top with an orange jacket. She appeared determined and sophisticated. She walked straight towards us and shook my hand.

"Bors," she said.

"Parastu, this is Frau Bors," Siawash introduced us to one another.

"*Frau* is used for women and *Herr*[13] for men followed by their last names," Arash had explained on our first trip to Viersen. "Also, do not call someone older than you by their first name unless you get permission."

The hallway jammed with joyful noises, all students getting to their classes. The two-story building had classes on both levels.

---

[13]   The title to address men in the German language

The laughter, playfulness, and exuberance of boys and girls took me back to my time in high school.

Back home, girls and boys studied separately from grade nine to twelve. Girls were dressed all in black uniforms, either dresses or skirts, and a top with black nylon. We also had to wear a white scarf. Boys didn't have any uniforms. I used to wear my white scarf around my neck with a black top and skirt, then I braided my hair on both sides with the traditional bangs. When the bell rang for first class we unwillingly entered class, ending our friendly chats.

Frau Bors faced Siawash and said, "I will meet with Parastu three times a week around noon."

"Great, Frau Bors. She will be at school to meet with you," Siawash replied. "Parastu is very excited to begin learning the language."

My right hand fiddled with my hair while my left clutched my thigh. My gaze travelled from face to face, understanding only my name. Frau Bors asked Siawash, "Is everything clear? We should get to class."

She turned to me and moved forward for another handshake.

"Parastu, don't feel lonely. I am here for you." She left for her class and Siawash turned to me.

"I will see you at home, sister."

A wave of soundlessness wallowed in the hallway that left me staring. I wandered towards the entrance and exited out onto Main street. The city was muted, or I'd turned deaf. The arriving bus displayed the town's name and I sat down, silently pleading. Tears threatened to burst but I stopped them from leaving my orbit. I didn't want my drama in the open. The bus stopped close to our apartment and I got off and started strolling. An air of nostalgia entered my lungs. I breathed in the hope of my parents on the other side of the globe. I didn't know if we shared the same oxygen, but I wanted to be free of the alienation I felt.

I realized that Siawash and I had left the apartment before 8 a.m., and a sudden anticipation for my parents' letter drew me to the mailbox. I ran to the door and opened the box, full of hope. It was empty. My estrangement grew. I missed home.

I took the stairs to our apartment on the third floor and slowly whispered a song to myself. The song was *Shanehayat Ra Baraye Gerye Kardan Dost Daram* or *Love Your Shoulder for Crying* by Hayedeh, an Iranian singer. My eyes welled with tears. I put the key in the door and entered the apartment. I sat on the couch, leaned my head on the sofa's arm, and closed my eyes in hopes of waking up at home.

I started taking classes with Frau Bors on her break three times a week, one-on-one tutoring. Frau Bors spoke with the school principal and got me in as a non-degree visiting student. I could sit in on classes, mainly language classes, with no expectation of homework or class participation.

On the first day as a visiting student, I was approached by my classmates. Some of the girls and boys walked to my chair and introduced themselves and made small talk. I returned home jubilant, my head held high that I'd made friends. The following week Arash and our cousins visited us. I told them about my progress and that I'd made some friends. They started laughing at me.

"Hamshira Jaan," Arash said, "No friendships develop just from greetings. It only lasts one day. It's not like back home when you say hi and someone becomes your best friend."

Frau Bors and I grew into a more substantial relationship. She became an anchor, like both a mother and big sister to me. She invited me to her home and introduced me to her own mother. I got to know her in-depth and discovered she had an immense passion for visual arts.

Together a visit to the Cologne Cathedral was arranged on a Saturday morning. Frau Bors showed me around the city, took me to different churches and historical places, and explained past events and the designs on the ceilings. It was awe-inspiring architecture. Frau Bors was very fond of education. One Sunday afternoon, when she'd invited me to her house in Neiderkrüchten, she opened up about her life.

It was a rich day. Nature manifested the fresh aroma of floral blooms as brilliant rays of sunshine settled on the warm earth. The poetic girl inside me wanted to be wrapped in verse and prose and dance upon the heath.

Frau Bors picked me up from my apartment and we stopped at a bakery near her house, and she purchased different slices of cakes. When we arrived at her home, she parked her car in the garage, and I went inside to greet her mother. She owned a ranch-style house with two bedrooms.

As we entered, the garage led us to an entrance that opened into a room with a skylight in the roof. We entered the kitchen and she put the cakes on the kitchen table. Coffee was served in the living room. The room was extensive, with a desk and chair facing a glass wall. On one side of the room was a wall-to-wall bookshelf, while three sofa pieces sat at the other end. A large window opened out to the yard with an illustrious small garden. The lilac tree branches bent over the fish-pond in the middle of the yard and were surrounded by different flowers—the clear work of a sophisticated gardener.

I valued how practical and classic Frau Bors was; she served each meal with its formal ritual. Afternoon tea had its own traditional ceremony. She covered the coffee table with a handmade tablecloth and used her fine china set and silver utensils for coffee. Then she announced that coffee was served and all three of us sat around the table, indulging in cake and freshly brewed coffee. The sun brushed through the window and touched us with its streams. Then her mother grew tired and left to take a nap and we wished her well.

I complied with Frau Bors's formality and routine and I started to look up to her and learn.

"Parastu, don't put your elbows on the dining table," she advised. I was eager to learn everything.

Frau Bors noticed my improvement and said, "Parastu, you are progressing really well. I'm proud of you."

As I talked, she corrected my sentences and encouraged me to talk more. I was comfortable enough to ask her personal questions.

"Frau Bors, please tell me about your childhood and youth. I want to know about your past," I said, "I want to know how you became a teacher."

She smiled. "Oh, Parastu," she said. Before starting a deep conversation, she always mentioned my name. She knew that I was still struggling with the language so she spoke slowly and stopped in the middle of the story asking, "Parastu, hast du alles verstanden, was ich gesagt habe?" *Did you understand everything*

I said? It amazed me how much she cared to define new words with present and past tense.

"Parastu, do you want more coffee?" she asked.

"No, thank you, Frau Bors."

"I schooled for eight years in our village at Neiderkrüchten. I was thirteen years old when the second world war was over. Our city was occupied by Britain and Britain's forces, and English was the language spoken at the offices. This is how I started learning English." She stopped, paused a little and continued, "In those days, a lady by the name of Mrs. Bieber—she was a doctor—moved to our village from one of the big cities in Germany, and she was fluent in English. Later, she taught me English and encouraged me to continue further education and enrolled me in one of our village's best high schools. After the entrance exam, I enrolled in the Faculty of Pedagogy at the University of Aachen." She paused, "Ist bisher alles klar?" she asked. *Is everything clear so far?*

"Of course Frau Bors," I answered.

She looked at me and smiled. "I know, Parastu. You are a brilliant and fine lady." She continued, "I was born on June 14th, 1932. My father was an electrical engineer. One day while he was working, someone turned on the lights by mistake, and as a result my father lost his life. That was 1933. I was seventeen months old, and my sister was three years old. My mother was widowed at a young age and took full responsibility for us. My mother is originally from Holland, but by 1939 she was not allowed to go to Holland and visit her family because of the onset of war. Despite my mom's relatives living just twenty kilometers from the German border, we were not supposed to cross the border to visit them." She sighed and hesitated, then looked at me. "Do you have to be home soon? I can drive you back any time you wish."

"No, Frau Bors, I want to know the rest of your story."

She continued, "Even after World War II ended in 1945, we were still restricted from visiting family. It took us several years to finally get permission to cross the border. Our life was tough in those days, but thank God we were still alive at the war's end. Slowly, our life started moving in a better direction. Over the years, I have met kind people. You are one of them."

Her face lit up with a beautiful smile. I leaned back in the sofa, impressed by her story. Her ascension in life warmed my essence, and her honor further impressed me as I discovered how she'd stood on her own through so many trials.

The sun was making its round and hushed elsewhere, but the summer afternoon was still young and brisk.

"Thank you, Frau Bors, for telling me your story," I said. "Can I ask you one last question for the day?"

"Aber naturlich," she said. *Of course.*

"Frau Bors, how did you find out about me?"

"When Siawash introduced himself to me he mentioned that he was Arash's brother, and I was Arash's language teacher for two years. I asked Siawash if he had any other siblings and Siawash said he had a sister." She continued, "I asked Siawash, 'How come your sister is not registered in school?' I was curious if it was because of gender differences. But Siawash said, 'My sister is nineteen years old and we don't know if she can join secondary school.'" Frau Bors paused, "Parastu, I wanted you to get the same education as Arash and Siawash."

I thought of Rumi, the Persian poet, chanting his great poem all around me. In one verse, he touches on the tale of Diogenes, the philosopher who said, "I lit a lamp in broad daylight and said, as I went about, I am searching for a human being."

We got up and started cleaning the coffee cups and plates, and then Frau Bors drove me back to my place. On the way home, we drove by fascinating green landscapes. It was a splendid view where the sky kissed the grass. Azure and emerald held us in their grip. I rolled down the window, the fragrant breeze caressing my soul. While I embraced new ideas with exuberance, an ill feeling of war suddenly buzzed around my head. The memory of childhood fought with adolescence and adulthood. My eyes landed on Frau Bors's mom then Frau Bors, and then back to the window. I leaned to my right, enchanted by nature and its virtue.

We entered the city of Viersen.

"Parastu, you were quiet, why?" Frau Bors asked. I told her I was enjoying the scenery. She parked near our apartment. Before getting out of the car, I turned to her mother and thanked her.

"It was an amazing afternoon; thank you, Frau Bors," I said. I got out of the car and waited, waving until the car disappeared in the distance. On our little trips with long drives I always enjoyed the serenity created by Frau Bors. She always sang out loud and asked me to join.

"Parastu, let me hear a song in your language, sing please," she would tell me.

"Amaday dir bad zod chera mirawi, ta ba sahar gomeshko bash koja miraw," I began singing a song my father loved so much and used to whisper around the house.

"Parastu what does it mean?" Frau Bors asked as she swayed her head to the rhythm.

"You came after so long, why leave so soon, stay until dawn, don't leave," I translated.

I grew closer with our neighbors. The building we lived in had three floors, like the other apartments in the neighbourhood. Each level had two flats on either side. We were living on the third floor, and our apartment was on the right. On the left side was a German woman who lived alone. Her name was Frau Schultz. Frau Schultz was in her mid-forties, almost my height, and had a pleasantly plump figure. She had short, dark-blond hair which always looked well-groomed. Frau Schultz always wore an apron over her dress when she was home.

Arash introduced me to her when we ran into one another on the stairs the first week I'd moved in. I started greeting her with simple hellos. Later, I learned to include the time of day in my greeting. As my German got better, we exchanged a few more sentences. And slowly I became acquainted with the people who lived on the first and second level, only by greeting them. But I grew the closest with Frau Schultz.

It started when Siawash and I left the house key at home one morning after leaving for school. Because of this, we had to buzz someone to get in. We buzzed Frau Schultz and she let us into the building and called the landlord to come and open the apartment for us.

"I suggest making an extra key," Frau Schultz said, "And if you like, you can leave it with me in case of emergency." She realized we were young and that it might happen again. And it did on numerous occasions. Finally, we made an extra copy of the key and left it with Frau Schultz for times of distress.

The apartment we lived in had a very specific housekeeping rule. The building administrator demanded all tenants clean the hallway between the two flats and the stairs once a week. Frau Schultz took the liberty to clean the hallway each week without asking Arash or our cousin. After I moved into the apartment, not the first couple of months, more towards the end of the second month, I realized this was the policy. She did it all by herself to help my brothers. I suggested to Frau Schultz that I help clean, sweep, and mop the hallway and stairs whenever it was our turn.

Frau Schultz invited me to her apartment for coffee. We talked about random stuff like my homeland and the war that had dominated for decades, or my parents. She was a seamstress who earned her living by taking orders and sewing for customers. I didn't know how to sew or take care of ripped clothes or mend zippers or do hemming. Whenever I needed help with tailoring, she was right there for me.

In the second year after my arrival to Viersen, my aunt's friend invited me, and not Siawash, to her daughter's wedding. I could choose a dress from the outfits I brought from home, but my heart fancied something unique. After my arrival and my engagement falling through, this was the first time I'd be attending a reception with the chance to dress up. I truly craved an elegant gown. I talked to Frau Schultz and she offered to make me a dress from a catalogue of my choice. All she asked was that I just pay for the fabric.

One big difference between our two cultures is that negotiations are an intimate thing. In my culture, if someone says no, it really means yes. We never settle on one answer, yes or no. We keep repeating the questions. Establishing an agreement right away is considered disrespectful.

I agreed upon the fabric payment. I reflected on a memory from my youth as it danced through my head. My mother and I had visited the tailor whose shop was near our house and went fabric shopping, followed by a restaurant meal. We went to a cousin's wedding and I eyed the latest styles. I wore red velvet pants and a top with a black tide cuff sleeve. My hair hung below my shoulders and a fancy headband rested on my forehead.

Frau Schultz and I scanned through the catalogue for dresses. My eyes found a two-piece dress with a full-length, flared satin skirt in light taupe and a fitted burgundy, velvet jacket. I chose that, and the next day we both went fabric shopping.

"We will pick you up at around five in the afternoon," Auntie called the morning of the party. It was an hour drive. I started getting ready and at 4:30 glanced in the mirror for the last inspection, a vast grin spreading from ear to ear.

Before going downstairs, I rang Frau Schultz's doorbell. She opened the door and her eyes examined me from top to bottom.

"You look beautiful, Parastu," she said.

The pleasant aroma of fresh cut flowers mingled with the perfume of guests as they arrived in groups and circled the atmospheric banquet hall. Close family members of the bride and groom were escorted to their seats. We were guided to a table occupied by some of Auntie and Uncle's friends. I greeted them and took my spot in a chair facing the ballroom, not the stage. I was not interested in their conversation and I let my eyes travel in an orbit for a familiar face. I was thirsty for a close friend, the party arousing nostalgia. The city of Viersen was tiny and not many Afghans lived here.

The engagement party was held in Bonn, a city with lots of immigrants. As I was scrutinizing faces, to my surprise, I recognized two people from home. My pulse started racing, and I moved from my chair without excusing myself and paced across the floor. The drum was beating in a short, rhythmic pattern, inviting guests to dance. I stepped in the opposite direction, and with each drumbeat, I moved faster until I met the arm of a friend from high school.

Teardrops stained our make-up, yet we grinned sentimentally. The other familiar face was Jebran's, a young man and family friend I knew well. We both relived our past and recalled our families.

"I am leaving for Canada soon," he said then hesitated, "I heard that you ended your engagement. How are you doing?"

I answered as many questions as I could, and he asked for my phone number.

"I wish you all the best on your new journey to Canada, and keep in touch," I said, and we parted.

Even though I was finding my way in this unfamiliar new world with Frau Bors's support, deep down, a voiceless void cried for more. The noise yearned for higher education, to attend university, but I could not phrase it aloud. It breathed only as a dream. I was still a refugee awaiting a second chance.

Chapter Five

It was the spring of 1990 or Nowruz[14] of 1369, in Kabul, Afghanistan. I cherished the tradition of the New Year back home. We always enjoyed the home-cooked meal of Sabzi Chalau, a rice and spinach dish, and Haft Mewa, a compote of seven fruits preserved in boiled water several days before Nowruz and served in its own juice. Gifts of new clothes and money from elders were the highlights of Sal-e-Now, New Year. Father was so proud of his ancestors and cultural celebrations, especially Nowruz. He took pride in teaching the history of Nowruz along with the other four ancient festivals Chaharshanbe Suri, Sizdah Be-dar, Mehregan, and Sadeh. He encouraged me to read aloud the famous poem *Beharya*, meaning spring, by Qahani, a Persian poet, which illuminated the new season's blossoms in its verses. Father would say, "Each line of this piece is like a rapture of the mind, bound with creativity and beauty."

"Siawash, Happy Nowruz!" I said. "I'm going to the city center, do you want to join me after school to eat out and celebrate the New Year?" My voice was elated by the word *new*. Earth was celebrating its rebirth, and I wanted to renew my own soul with a fresh start.

I dressed in jeans with a white blouse and a blue shawl draped over one shoulder. The bracing climate caressed me and whispered a soft hello. A scented aroma of spring buds in the air performed a promise. The rhythmic chirping of birds stirred the poet inside me. I walked along the store-lined main street, enjoying the crowds. I loved being around people. Seeing people enter a flower shop, a grocery, or a clothing store was evidence of life still moving. Life was truth, not a mirage.

I finished the main street's first stroke by entering the bus stop and walking towards the end of Aldi's grocery shop. I turned around and drifted back to the main shopping area. I strolled along the two sides of boutiques, entering some to explore new styles. I didn't have extra money to shop, only browse. I drew closer to the shop where I'd seen the salesclerk waving on my first week in this strange land. As I passed by, I hoped she was working. I arrived at the front of the store and stopped to have a look inside.

"Guten tag!" *Good day*, a voice said, heading my way. A woman walked towards me as I stepped inside the store. She wore a solid purple skirt and was slim with short blonde hair. Maybe it was a trend in those days.

"Guten Morgen," *Good morning*, she said, followed by "Wie geht es dir?" *How are you?* I replied, "Guten morgen, ich bin gut, danke." *I am good, thank you.* Then I asked, "Wie geht es ihnene?" *How are you?* Out of respect, I changed the pronoun.

"I am good too," she said and smiled, "And by the way, I'm Anna," and held out her hand for a handshake.

"I am Parastu."

"Do you work on this street?" Anna asked.

"No, I don't. I only take German language classes," I added.

She looked at me thoughtfully and asked, "Do you want to work?"

Without hesitation, I answered "Yes."

It was the first time I'd considered working instead of studying. I immediately asked myself if my desolation was so transparent that people around me pitied me. This was my first introduction to work. It felt like my rib cage was expanding in size, like I could inhale all the air around me, keep gasping, and still have space for more.

I quickly brought my attention back to the conversation.

Anna continued, "A few blocks down the street, a coffee/restaurant shop is looking for a dishwasher. If you like," she said, "I will ask them to meet with you tomorrow. I know them."

I feared if I asked why she was interested in helping me, it would offend her.

So I only said, "Yes." There was no need to think about it.

"Do you have time now? I could take you there to arrange an appointment?"

Anna asked one of her coworkers to watch the store and we walked to the restaurant located on the opposite side of city center transit station. It was a small coffee/restaurant shop with only four or five tables, with large windows that covered the front and side of the shop. They served breakfast and dinner. We entered the shop and Anna introduced me to the lady working there and arranged the interview. Then Anna went back to the clothing

store, and I headed towards my aunt's apartment to tell everyone the news.

UNIVERSITY. I TOOK A big breath in as sweat rushed to my back. I
walked, felt the paved road with each step. A new revelation came
to me as a cold howl whipped through the spring blossoms. I so
much longed to be where Arash was, at university.

One minute I was happy, the next, I returned to my prima-
ry concern. I thought I would be the navigator of my destiny.
Why couldn't I give voice to my inner wishes? Words escaped
my mind. I disguised myself as a warrior, but inside I felt like
an underdog.

I screamed on paper with mind-blowing words and cried on
the shoulders of my diaries.

Mom and Dad wrote to Arash, Siawash and Auntie, "Parastu
is vulnerable and a very sensitive girl, please be mindful of her."

"Parastu is a very strong girl," they replied, "Do not worry
about her. She studies the language and in her leisure time with
Sahar[15], we hear them laughing."

Finding a job, my first job with the help of a complete stranger,
was well received. I had no idea how to look for a job, nor did I
know if it was even possible with my refugee status. I did not
even know my rights, or that a human being had rights. What
were rights?

The following day, I got ready and took the bus to the restaurant for my interview. My uncle agreed to meet me there. I met
him at the corner of the clothing store and together we walked

15   *Sahar* means *dawn*

to the shop. The manager introduced herself. She was shorter than me with black hair and an average build. It was my very first experience with job interviews. I had no idea how it would go. The manager invited us to the back of the store. We sat down and she asked me a few questions. I answered as much as I could, given my understanding of the language. My uncle was there for support.

The manager said they needed someone to be at the restaurant from 5 p.m. until 9 or 10 p.m., five days a week to help wash dishes and assist the cook. She offered ten marks of German money and I accepted the offer. Right away, I thought of my cousin Sahar who was in the same situation I was.

Sahar and I basically grew up together. We were best friends, though we were two completely different characters. She was average in height and weight with short hair and dark eyebrows, which made her face even prettier. Sahar was fearless. One common interest that intrigued us both was a love for poetry and books. She'd arrived in Germany before me and lived with her brother in a different city just a thirty minutes' bus ride away. I asked the manager if she could work two nights, and I work three nights.

She accepted. "Bring your cousin next time. When can you start?"

"I can start tomorrow night," I said. We shook hands and said goodbye.

I was happy with my decision to bring Sahar and handling the interview well. I thanked my uncle for being there and said goodbye to him. I also wanted to let Anna know of my decision.

The day of any new start was followed by a struggle of happy yet somber feelings.

I was supposed to be at work around 5 p.m., but by 2 p.m., I was ready. I walked around the city to kill time, and at 4:30, I entered the restaurant.

"Good afternoon," I said to the lady who was working. "I am Parastu."

"Good afternoon. I'm Emma," she said. "You're early," she emphasized.

Emma walked with me to the shop's back, where a door opened to a storage room. The room was small with shelves around it, close to the ceiling, and a wall-mounted coat rack near the door. She showed me where to leave my purse and jacket. She emphasized that everything we needed for the front was stored there.

We walked back to the front, where a freestanding, stain-less-steel double sink faced the restaurant's back. The front was divided by a transparent wall where a food preparing station was. A cash register sat beside the food stand facing the front wall. Emma explained that my job was to clean tables and wash dishes. Emma and I worked together for three nights, and then Sahar would work with a different cook.

Sahar and I were good friends. On our days off, we got to-gether and discussed our new jobs, laughing about the mistakes caused by the language barrier. While Siawash and the cousins decided to go out on a Saturday afternoon, I called Sahar and asked her to come for a sleepover. She came and I made Korma

Chalau Badenjanroomy[16], a white rice with tomato korma, and one of our favorite dishes. In the kitchen, I set up the table for two. The kitchen was narrow but long, the window welcoming natural light. Sahar and I settled into our seats and satisfied our appetite with our heavenly dish, spellbound by work stories.

"One busy night at the restaurant," I started, "Emma asked me to fetch her flour from the back. I didn't know what she meant, but my ego stopped me from asking. I went into the storage room, assuming I would be able to find what she asked for, or it would show up right before my eyes, and I would be able to recognize it. I was wrong. I looked around and around at the storage room and could not find it while it was right in front of me. I went back and told her, 'I cannot find it.' She just shook her head and went herself to the back to find it."

We both started laughing. Most of the time, we ended up crying for our parents, reminiscing about the past, and feeling gloomy about our present circumstances. One night after crying so much about our shattered desires, we both confessed something to each other.

"I wish someday I will have a boy, not a girl, since I do not want my girl to suffer as I suffered," Sahar said.

"I want to have a girl," I said, "I would let my daughter live free and experience everything I missed in life."

I went to school in the morning and worked in the evening. After a month of working at the restaurant, the manager handed us our salaries, but it was not the amount we had discussed at the interview. I finished my shift and went home. The next day I

---

16   Curry made with tomato sauce and pot roast, served over white rice

called Sahar to discuss the problem with our wages. She agreed we'd been paid less.

"We should stand up for what was promised," I suggested.

She disagreed with me. "I am not going to say anything."

The following day, I confronted the manager. She opposed the ten marks per hour and I resigned, but I did not want to concern Anna with what had happened.

One of the clothing stores on the busy street of Hauptstraße needed a salesclerk. I saw the sign for help wanted displayed in the store's front window as I passed to get to the bus station. The following day, I decided to go inside the store and ask in person if I could work there. I dressed up in casual clothes as usual, jeans with a button-up shirt and white runners. I left my hair down in a natural-looking wave. The bus stopped at the central station, and I walked towards the clothing shop. I opened the glass door and noticed that the store was much larger inside than it looked from the outside. Clothes were displayed everywhere, with wall-mounted racks on both sides of the store. It had clothes mostly for middle-aged women.

I walked right up to the salesclerk at the cash register in the middle of the store. The lady at the cash register was in her mid-fifties and short with short blond hair, and wore glasses. She was busy doing something at the register. There were also other clerks, but they were busy helping customers. I approached the counter with a smile on my face.

"Good morning, I would like to apply for the salesclerk position," I said.

The lady raised her head and scanned me thoroughly with a sharp look.

"Oh, do you?" she asked as her harsh tone spread around me. Her peculiar gaze landed on my face and back to the cash register. She played with her facial expressions a little bit, taking her time to answer. She opened her mouth as her look shouted directly at mine and said, "We have no position available for foreigners."

The word foreigner dumped over me like a bucket of ice-cold water, and I froze. My long hair jumped to my rescue. It covered my face and whispered to me not to meet the salesclerk's eyes. A sudden desire for a set of wings arrested my heart. I forced my numb body towards the door at once and walked straight to the bus stop. Every single muscle in my body had one objective: to get home.

In the summer of the same year, I was on the bus going home one midafternoon, sitting at the very back seat of the bus, deep in my own thoughts with grocery bags in my lap. The bus was relatively empty. There were only a few middle-aged men and women and five school-aged boys. Two were sitting and the rest stood holding the bar close to one another. I was the only immigrant.

The bus stopped at a few stations and resumed moving.

A phrase, "Foreigners, out of our country. Foreigners, out, out, out of our country," chanted around the bus. I looked away from the window to see who the alien was. I saw myself at the center of five sets of eyes, staring at me with all the nerves and muscles in their heads.

Ding. My finger pressed the stop button without a second thought and I extricated my dark brown skin and hair off the bus. I walked the rest of the way to the apartment carrying the groceries. I took the short cut by the pond and forest. It was silent in nature. *Has she heard of my embarrassment?* I wondered. My ego and pride were singing with longing. The forest stillness encouraged the words to seep out of my mouth. With each step I took I grew louder and louder until I heard the echo of my voice traveling through each branch of the trees and banging on the ground, screaming, "Who am I? Where is my home?"

＊＊

ANNA INTRODUCED ME TO the world of employment, and I wanted to continue working. After quitting the dishwashing position, I tried to fill positions in supermarkets. For each job I had to get permission from the refugee office. I didn't know where the office was but the managers took the duty upon themselves to get me the authorization. I also applied for newspaper deliveries.

I called Sahar. "Let's do newspaper delivery! It won't to take too much of our time if we just do it around our neighborhood." She agreed.

The next day Sahar and I visited the office. We signed up and gave our address for a monthly pay of twenty-five marks, starting the following week. The next week I noticed that I'd received only one newspaper per day.

I called Sahar, "I'm receiving only one paper a day, what is going on? Let's go back to the office."

"Ma'am you subscribed to receive a newspaper daily," the gentleman in the office said.

"I am so sorry, there has been a misunderstanding, we wanted to deliver newspapers, not receive them," I explained.

"Okay, no worries, just return the paper and we will take you off our subscription list." He kindly dismissed us.

⁂

AS A NON-DEGREE VISITING student, I watched my classmates prepare for graduation. Fifteen- and sixteen-year-old boys and girls, giggling and glowing, were impatient to leave Realschule for their future. Some were heading to high school, but most were doing the Ausbildung, a type of vocational schooling.

A few weeks before graduation, during my study time with Frau Bors, she asked me, "Parastu, do you want to do Ausbildung? Do you want to pursue a career?"

The pen in my hand dropped and landed on the paper. To my astonishment, Frau Bors laid open the hidden desire before me. The word "studying" thrilled my existence, and I trembled with inspiration. Excitement made me tongue-tied.

"Frau Bors, is that possible?" I asked, wide-eyed.

"You did finish grade twelve in your country, and you were in the second year of university, isn't that right?"

"Yes."

"Do you have any documents from your university and high school?" she asked.

"I have my grade twelve documents but not the university since I only finished three semesters when I left home," I answered immediately.

"Can you bring your twelfth-grade certificate to our next meeting? I'll send it to the school board and see if it gets accepted by them, and we'll take it from there."

With both arms in the air, I drifted on my toes. A happy poem flowed around the room, and I danced to the opposite side of the table, hugging Frau Bors. Droplets of tears ran to my neck.

"Parastu, are you crying?" Frau Bors's voice put me back in my seat.

"I am excited. I am excited," I continued, "Thank you, Frau Bors."

Chapter Six

International news broadcasted the decay of Afghanistan's war; civilians tried to escape to any country they could on the world map.

One day Siawash said, "Sister, a new Afghan refugee family relocated to Viersen and their boys are in our school. Let's visit them and invite them over for dinner."

I cooked Pulao rice[17] and potato curry. In our culture cooking rice is a must with any dinner invitation, especially pulao. A party without pulao is considered an offense towards guests.

The family brought an abundance of stories of the war and how people had been consumed by fear. An ambiguous thought kept me in dread that night. I just wanted to hear Mom and Dad's voice and hear they were fine and doing okay.

Calling home was a challenge, considering the power outages and telecommunication troubles. For my parents to contact us from home was a colossal undertaking. They had to go to the telecommunication center and request a call to Germany and present them with the number. Then, the center would connect them from their end with a limited time. The other option was

---

17   A staple dish made with basmati rice and aromatic herbs

bribery. Or, if you had a connection within the government, your issue would be solved with a simple phone call.

The power outages had been an ongoing problem since the beginning of the war. Seldom did people have power twenty-four hours a day, seven days a week, due to the lack of power. The power posts were bombed down by either the Mujahedeen or the government, so the power distribution for each household was controlled by the electricity center of that particular town. Each household in Kabul was given turns to have power. It was only two or three times a week, day or night.

My brain recalled a memory from my teenage years in Karte Parwan[18], and I grinned, my eyes closed for a mental image. It was a Thursday night around 6 p.m., with the announcer introducing the outline of the evening. At precisely 6 p.m., I called Siawash to the family room so we could listen together. Siawash ran upstairs while I turned the TV on.

The speaker's voice travelled around the room, "Good evening everyone."

The narrator broke down the evening's scheduled programs by the hour and finally got to the main event. "Tonight's movie is *Amar, Akbar and Anthony* at 9 p.m." It was an Indian movie with a Farsi-Dari voiceover that we loved to watch.

Siawash and I started dancing and radiating joyful noises to the entire house. I ran downstairs, giggling and yelling, "Bebe Jaan! Bebe Jaan!"

I stopped for more breathing and said, "Tonight's movie is *Amar, Akbar and Anthony*!" Siawash joined me, and we

---

18   Karte Parwan is a city in Kabul

both put our hands in the air and sang, "Amarrrr, Akbarrrr, Anthoooooony."

We all returned to different rooms, and I sat down behind my desk to write in my diary. Then, I saw the lights go off, and I was alone in the dark.

"No way!" I screamed. Siawash and I were on our hands and knees, praying for the power to return. It did not.

By 8:30 p.m., we'd lost all hope and, with long faces, headed to bed. Frustration put me into a deep sleep, when a voice penetrated our bedroom.

It was Mom announcing, "Power is back on! Get up watch your movie."

"What time is it?" I asked Mom while pushing the comforter off.

"Nine thirty," Mom said.

We both jumped out of bed, ran to the living room, turned on the TV, and watched the show, which had started thirty minutes earlier. The film was over at midnight, and ironically the power went back off. The enjoyment of that evening was significant, but the power outage remained a mystery.

"Guten morgen," I said to the first-floor neighbor the next day as I climbed the stairs. I had only German class first in the morning, but my mind was in conversation with Mom and Dad. I picked up the phone handset, and before dialing the number I counted the time in Kabul. It was a three-hour time difference.

I hung up. Mom was not home. I went back to the kitchen to make myself lunch.

Four. Five. It was six in the evening in Kabul, Afghanistan, I reassured myself. My index finger traveled in a circle twelve times on the rotary phone and with each digit I touched I said, "Please God, let the call go through."

I heard the phone ring once, twice. Three rings competed with my heart beats but before a fourth I heard, "Bali Befarmayed." *Hello. Please go ahead.*

It was Dad. All of a sudden, I noticed the softness of the carpet beneath my bare feet.

"Padar Jaan. Salaam, Parastu astom[19]," I used the title for Father, something I used to call him before introducing myself. I could not stop crying.

Whenever I called home, I had to keep in mind what was said and the time limit. Back home, every conversation was inspected by the authorities. The time was given by the switchboard and we could not surpass it. So, I had to organize a list of things to be discussed before the connection.

"Why are you crying? We are good like flowers." It was a slang phrase. My father continued, "Tell me about yourself, Arash, and Siawash."

"They're both doing great with their studies." I answered, "Dad, I also have good news. I will go to school to study with the support of Frau Bors." They knew about Frau Bors. I had told them about her in a letter. My father always said, "Never forget someone's support and goodness."

"Great news, my daughter," he said. The blessing in his voice bounced through my physique.

Quickly, before the line could get cut off, I asked, "Dad, can I talk to Mom?"

19　Term meaning *I am*

He hesitated then said, "She is not home. She is working late." Then with a laugh, continued, "Here she is, she just arrived!"

A frail voice answered me, "Parastu Jaan, my daughter, how are you?"

"Bebe Jaan, are you good? Is Grandma Bebe Kalan fine?"

The line cut off and left me with an abundance of questions.

I suspected they were hiding something from me. So, without any further reasoning, I called Aunt Razia. Auntie answered the phone.

"Salaam, Auntie," I said, and promptly asked, "Is Mom okay? Is Grandma fine?" I explained the conversation I'd just had with them.

"Calm down," she said. "A couple of weeks ago we received a letter from your father that your mother Perwin was very ill. They were worried and asked us not to mention it to you guys." She continued, "We have been in touch and she's recovered, but still very feeble."

The bell rang, the jarring sound shook my thoughts that had dwelled on Mom's illness since last night. I left German class and walked downstairs to go to the meeting room. The sparkling vibrations of young students moving around the building sounded like a heartbeat flatline to my ears. I opened the door, the natural light that shined through the window was too sharp. I arrived before Frau Bors and chose the chair where my back could face the window. Frau Bors entered and made herself comfortable. Reaching for her briefcase, she took out the textbook we were working on, and laid it on the desk.

She looked at me with a smile and said, "Wie geht es dir? Hast du dein zeugnis mit gebracht?" *How are you Parastu? Did you bring your report card with you?*

Without further delay, I answered, "Frau Bors, Frau Bors," My voice trembled, "I want to go back home," I said, and tears poured down my face. She leaned forward on the chair, her brows furrowed.

"Parastu is something wrong? What happened?"

I explained my phone call to home and Mom being sick and how much I missed them. She grabbed my hands from across the desk and her eyes spoke.

"Parastu, do you understand why your parents sent you off to Germany? To survive the war and start a better life." She answered as she asked the question and continued, "Do you know that you will cause them more suffering than joy with your return? You should stay here, go to school, stand on your own feet, make a future for yourself, and bring them over." She sighed and continued, "It is your turn to help them, not the other way around."

Tears stopped dropping. My cold palms and fingers twisted and her voice resonated. *To help them and bring them over.* The idea offered the promise of us six under one roof to my restless being.

"Frau Bors, I will bring the report card tomorrow."

There were only a few days left in the school year before summer holidays. At the bus stop near school, I took the bus to the Monchengladbach city center. I didn't want to wait for the Viersen bus. At the intersection of our street and the main road, I pressed stop. I strolled, taking pleasure in the fresh, mild breeze.

A tiny bakery with a fascinating cake display in the window caught my eye. The shop stood alone in the middle of apartments and a desire to inspect the cakes lured me to the glass. As I was admiring the assorted loaves and praising the detail of fruits and edible flower toppings, I saw in the bottom corner of the window a pink piece of paper that read, "Help wanted for a baker on Sundays." In Viersen, Germany, working on Sundays was uncommon, I understood. I valued my Sunday afternoon tradition of coffee and cake. Frau Bors and I met several times at her place for our Sunday coffee routine, dining like royalty.

Remembering the conflict of my previous experience though, I feared entering the shop. Instead, I jotted down the bakery's number. As soon as I got home, I called them.

A female voice answered, "Hello Bakery!"

I mentioned that I was looking for a job.

"Do you have time this afternoon to come in for an interview?" the woman asked.

"Sure," I said and brought my fist down in glory and hurried up to the kitchen.

I quickly prepared food for Siawash and I. Siawash had basketball practice after school, so I left him a note saying that I'd gone for a job interview and would explain more after coming home.

I switched my shirt to a white button-up and wore the same colour runners. Then I left the apartment and started walking to the store. When the bakery appeared in the distance, I took a deep breath. Then I exhaled and entered the store. The shop was divided into two sections by a glass showcase.

The baker behind the counter noticed me and, with a smile, asked, "What would you like?"

"I am Parastu. I have an interview for the posted position," I said.

She told me to wait a minute and headed to the back to inform the manager. She came back and lifted a small portion of the glass showcase so I could follow her through a door behind the counter.

A thin corridor took us to a hidden office. The room was packed to its capacity, papers on the desk, and a shelf loaded with books and folders. A woman in her late thirties with short, brown hair sat in the middle of the vast piles, facing a computer.

"Good afternoon," she said. She stood and shook my hand before she continued, "I'm Marie."

"Good afternoon. I am Parastu, " I replied.

"Thanks for coming in on such short notice Parastu. Am I pronouncing it correctly? Parastu, have a seat."

I took a seat. "Yes, you are pronouncing it correctly. And thanks for having me."

She sat back down in her seat behind the desk.

Marie began explaining the job description. "My intention is to open the store for two hours on Sunday afternoon due to the customer's queries. The position involves selling cakes and cookies, and I pay twenty-five dollars per hour, double wage." Then Marie asked, "Now let me hear about you, tell me about yourself."

I swallowed my breath down; I was debating with my rambling thoughts in skepticism; where should I start?

"My name is Parastu. I am from Kabul, Afghanistan. I'm twenty years old." I talked slowly, fishing for information. I didn't know how to define myself. I continued, "I live in Viersen, not far from here." I paused.

"When did you come to Germany?" she asked.

"Almost two years ago," I answered.

"Do you go to school? What are you studying?"

It took me by surprise that a complete stranger was interested in my life.

"I study the language only." I didn't know how far I could go with my personal life.

Marie studied me with tenderness and continued, "You are too young to be just working. You should go to school and have a career."

For a few seconds, I let the advice stir in my mind and I conversed with myself. *Is my confusion, status, and vulnerability so transparent? Should I explain my situation? Why is she concerned about my education?* My mind sparked at the word studying, my long-lived desire to go to university, have a higher degree education, attach a title beside my name. Desire flooded the wilderness of my spirit.

"I love to study. Education has been my focal point since I landed, but I do not know if I am entitled. I am only a refugee." I continued, "I have been helped with the language by my instructor. Right now, I'm a visiting student at Realschule, in grade ten." I swallowed and fixed my fleeting gaze at her face, "My twelfth-grade diploma from back home has been sent to the school board." The words choked in my throat, "For approval."

Haha! You are nobody. I heard the walls, the roof, the shelves, the light bulb that scattered light around the dark room, mock me as they danced before my eyes.

"Parastu," I heard Marie asking, "Would you like to go to school for baking, to do Ausbildung?"

I summoned myself, and directed my gaze at Marie.

She didn't wait for me to answer. "Parastu, I offer you the job. You can start this Sunday, if you want. And think about studying baking."

I was speechless and genuinely touched by her advice. I straightened my posture and said: "Vielen dank[20] for the job offer. I will start this Sunday." About Ausbildung, I sensed my own cold feet, a wave of uncertainty. "I am a refugee, so I don't know." I swallowed again, "I am confused about what to study since everything is new to me."

"Hold on a minute," Marie said, and she picked up the phone and dialed a number.

I did not know who she was calling, but I guessed it might be someone connected to refugees.

"Hello," Marie said and asked to be transferred to the Immigration and Refugee Department. After a few seconds of waiting, she said, "Guten tag. How are you? I am calling on behalf of a beautiful young girl who is sitting right in front of me, and she is a refugee from Afghanistan." She looked at me. "She is willing to study, but she does not know if she is permitted. Parastu," she said, while she covered the phone with her left hand, "Parastu, what is your last name and date of birth?"

I got up from my seat and grabbed a notepad, writing down my last name and date of birth before laying it down in front of Marie.

---

20   *Thanks very much*

Before sitting down I looked at door, goosebumps erupted all over my arms. A chilling scene played in my mind, layering fear in my heart. *She is a refugee. She is stateless. We will send her back to her own country.* The mental scene in my head screamed. *She will be imprisoned for leaving the country.* I pictured the police officers at the Kabul airport, shouting at me.

I sat down, pressing my feet into the floor and gripped my thighs in hopes the ground would open up and swallow me.

Marie's voice broke the silence, "Thank you, I really appreciate your support, sir." She hung up the phone and turned to me with a smile on her face. "Parastu," she hesitated and continued, "You are permitted to study. Congratulations!" Marie continued, "Let me know when your transcript gets approved, and if you decided to study baking, I can help arrange the schooling." You can start your part-time job this Sunday."

She rose from her seat and walked me to the front to introduce me to the girls. I stood tall as she said my name.

I shook her hand with a secure grip. "Thank you so much, Frau Marie. I will be here on Sunday! Goodbye!" I smiled at the other girls and left.

My runners touched the sidewalk and my feet felt the gentle strike of the concrete. Every step I took I grew lighter and lighter, and flew over the paved road. I heard a noise. It grew closer. *Who could it be?* I wondered. It was Hafiz reciting his ghazal[21] around me.

---

21 A lyrical style in poetry

"Amidst flowers, wine in hand,
   my lover I embrace,
   King of the world is my slave on such a day in
   such a place."

Then, Gibran Khalil Gibran joined and read his joy and sorrow poem. I hurried home.

Once, I wrote a prose poem about home.

What is Home? An original poem. I recite;

I wonder to see four walls arise from the ground to protect me from ills and threats. A home is where I can give birth to my free self. Home, a mother's arm, cradle my soul with tenderness. Home grounds my feet when I jump with triumph and cushion my head when I cry with sorrow. That's why I simply utter, "I want to go home," in any circumstances.

◆ ◆

SPRING WAS MORPHING INTO summer and I finished class with Frau Bors. I could taste the brightness and warmth of early summer in my mouth. I defined summer as freedom of mind and body. I also described it as a sunny day, diamonds descending from the sky. I shall go out and be able to catch the falling gems.

My feet asked my brain to serve the heart and travel to the city center. I hopped on the bus going into town. I walked the long way up the main street, entering a few stores to check for new styles. I stopped at an Italian ice cream shop in the middle of the road. The outdoor seats on a busy street were almost full so I ordered my favorite ice cream, Spaghetti Ice, at the register. It was a sin to sit inside, I said to myself.

I found an empty table with two chairs under an umbrella, inviting me in. The waiter brought my ice cream, put it on the table, and left.

I indulged my appetite for that sweet, cold vanilla ice cream shaped like spaghetti, covered with strawberry sauce. Heat enfolded me with its humidity. My hair landed heavily on my bare shoulders. My olive skin was tan from too many sunrays. I refused to cover my eyes with the dark shade of sunglasses. Instead, I set them free to scan the glare of sunlight with its natural beauty.

While nature's serenity scattered my frustration, a male voice grabbed my attention. "Excuse me, is this seat free? Can I sit?" Without waiting for an answer, he pulled up the chair and sat down.

I straightened my posture and ran my fingers through my hair, figuring he was probably just hunting for a seat to enjoy the outdoor glamour.

"I am sorry to intrude," he said, "I am Paul. What a beautiful day."

I slowly realized that his intention was not only for the seat.

"May I ask for your name?" he said.

I quickly looked around to see if anyone else witnessed this scene, but no one else was involved. Everyone minded their own business.

"I'm sorry, do I know you?" I asked.

He took me by surprise. I did not know what to say or do. Mainly, I was worried about an Afghan walking by and seeing me sitting with a man. Within a day, the news would be twisted and proclaimed throughout the city that Parastu had a German boyfriend.

I did not want to sound unintellectual or like a foreigner, so I kept my ego and let my back hug the chair.

"No, we do not know each other," he said, "But when you walked in here, I could not help but notice you. I had to come forward and introduce myself. I could not keep my eyes off you. I am sorry if I offended you." He ended his statement with a smile. He was a handsome young man in his mid to late twenties, tall, with dark blond hair.

I finally collected myself, "I am Parastu. Yes, it is a beautiful day."

"I am a pharmacist. I work on the next street."

I did not introduce myself further. I did not have anything else to add in any way. Who was I really? I had no country to claim, no career to profess. I was nobody, just a name. We exchanged a few pleasantries about the weather and the Italian shop. I finished my ice cream and got up.

"I'm sorry, I don't want to be rude, but I have to catch the bus," I said.

Paul got up and, from his wallet, pulled a card with his name and number on it. "Here is my card Frau Parastu. I work in town every day. I'd like to get to know you more, I insist. Please give me a call so I can take you out for lunch or dinner and get a chance to know you better."

I grabbed his card, shook his hand, and said goodbye.

On my way to the bus stop, I could not help but think about what just transpired and how handsome he was.

I noticed you as soon as you walked in.

I played his sentence over and over in my head. I smiled and turned to look at myself on every glass window I came across on the Hauptstraße.

At a very young age, a wish from my father was bestowed upon me for eternity. In grade ten, I got my report card. I'd gained the third-highest grade in the class and I brought it home. My father was on the upstairs balcony. The weather was warm, the terrace facing the Asmayee mountain. Cherry trees, standing tall around the front yard, transformed the afternoon heat into a pleasant, mild breeze. Mother always asked Gulali or one of us to furnish the balcony with the outdoor mat and rug before dinner.

I climbed the stairs and went straight to my father, very excited to show him my grades. He welcomed me with pride and kind words.

Celebrating my triumph he said, "Wow, wow my dearest. My daughter, this is amazing that you came third in your class and continue getting the highest marks. Well done, and I am proud of you." He added, "But one thing I wish from you, is to respect my name and standing in the society. Please remember to honor this." He handed me my report card and I promised I would respect his yearning. I went to my room and pondered on what he'd said.

In our culture, it's essential to honor the family's name and reputation. But the sad truth of our society was that men were treated much differently than women. Relationships for women were highly discouraged, while for men were celebrated.

The bus stopped near the apartment. I got off and wandered. I pushed gently, and with each step I demanded myself to abandoned a piece of Paul's card into the forgotten bin of my mind.

Chapter Seven

After almost two years of living in Viersen, Germany, I was granted a second trial for my immigration status. I received a letter with the date, time, and place for my interview.

In spring of 1991, Siaswash and I boarded a train leaving south from Viersen station early in the morning. Siawash missed school to accompany and give me moral support and to be my interpreter.

The little girl who dressed in white and lived in the garden of poetry was frozen for quite some time. She imagined the judge reading the verdict, "You cannot stay here, you should leave immediately." The sounds wrapped her senses, and she covered her ears. Yet, the dormant artist yearned so much to be a free citizen with the right to roar.

Before boarding the train in Viersen, I stopped in front of a cigarette vending machine, inserted change and pushed for a Marlboro light. *Weesh, weesh.* As the pack hit the bottom of the machine, a quick memory presented itself.

It was the end of March on the Easter long weekend and Arash had visited us from university. I invited cousins over for dinner and music. I informed my neighbors of the loud music and apologized for any noise in advance. Dinner was served at five in the afternoon. After we cleaned the dishes, we moved with our tea cups and sweets into the living room. We pushed the sofa and couch to the corners to make more space for the instruments. We all gathered on the floor. Arash and our cousins played the armonia and tabla while we sang. A pack of Marlboro cigarettes went around the circle and we each took one, lit it, and used a plate as ashtray. Siawash and Sahar's youngest brother were the only two people who did not smoke.

I played the role of Siawash's guardian and advised, "Smoking is bad for you and you are too young to smoke. I forbid you."

The beat of the lyrics filled the air. We swayed our heads to the wave of rhythm, puffs of smoke coiled around the sound. We joined the singer, singing the lyrics together. Young and carefree, the walls protected us and time smiled in the face of our serenity.

Jerr, Jerr! The doorbell rang. We all looked at one another. It was only eight in the evening. They stopped the music and I ran to the kitchen to see from the window who it could be. It was Uncle Gul, who'd come to visit Arash. We all dispersed into different rooms, pushing all the windows open. Someone used the tray to fan the air out the window. Someone else used air freshener, spraying it around the living room. The sofa and the couch were moved back to their original position. After a good five minutes we invited Uncle in.

Uncle's voice thickened as he bit his lips. "Smoking is bad for you guys," he lectured, "Do you guys want me to write to your parents of your disobedience?"

Drum. The Marlboro light dropped from the machine. Siawash looked at me.

"You know that I only smoke occasionally for pleasure, but today, I think I need it to calm my nerves," I pleaded.

Siawash befriended muteness, letting the sound of the train speak for him. Meanwhile, I was slicing through my thoughts to answer questions about my escape.

The train arrived at the destination. The court building appeared a short distance away. I trembled and lit a cigarette. Before that one was finished, I lit another one.

The meeting was a couple of hours, I answered all the questions and Siawash translated. The interviewer, before dismissing us, mentioned that the decision would be mailed to me. By the time it was over, it was around two in the afternoon and we headed back to the train station, checking the schedule. The next train was leaving in five minutes and we rushed to get on.

We blew in a gentle wind and occupied two seats next to each other. A high-pitched sound whistled as the door closed. We began telling stories of home and Germany. We were like a non-stop music channel. The sound of people talking, the smell of perfume, breath, sweat, and food, traveled around us. But nothing interrupted us, not even our empty stomachs. The last meal we'd had was the night before.

"Do you remember back home when I hid under the kitchen counter and scared Gulali by pinching her foot like a mouse?" Siawash asked.

We both burst into laughter, and he continued, "Gulali was smart though, and got back at me by pretending to faint. Do you remember how nervous I got? I kept saying to Gulali, 'Please wake up! I made a mistake. Please, I swear I won't do it again!'"

The train stopped at a few stations then resumed without disturbing our joyful stories. Then he confessed to a prank he'd pulled on me.

"On the evening the soccer world cup was broadcasted, I invited Mansoor for a sleepover." Mansoor was Sahar's youngest brother and the same age as Siawash. "You came home from work tired and wondered why Mansoor was sleeping over on a weeknight." He stopped for the train announcement and continued, "You made dinner for us three and we helped with the dishes and cleaning the kitchen, to help you finish faster. You made yourself tea, and then we sat around chatting. Then, to your surprise, you saw the clock and how late it was. You said, 'I cannot believe it's ten already. I have to work tomorrow!' You pointed at the clock and screamed and excused yourself." He smiled "We moved the clock one hour forward to watch the world cup."

"You did not?" I said with a hearty laugh. "Oh well! It's okay. I am not very fond of soccer anyway. The two sports I really like are ones I taught myself, bike riding and swimming," I said.

Siawash asked, "Really? That's interesting. How?"

"Sahar and I visited the swimming pool in the city one day. But we didn't know how to swim so we stayed at the edge of the pool. A group of boys and girls jumped in the pool and started racing, splashing, and giggling. Sahar and I looked at one another and asked what the big deal was about swimming. If they can do it, why can't we? We both held one hand on the edge of the pool and slowly moved our legs, and with the other hand, we pushed forward. On the next round, we let go and swam freely, but only in the shallow area. I also realized that I could go to school or the city center by riding a bicycle. So, I purchased a small, cheap bike from the flea market and practiced until I learned it."

"Oh yes, I remember," Siawash said, "Your junior bicycle! Your tall body hunched way over it." We both laughed.

"Viersen!" The announcer called. We clutched the handrail and the door swung open.

♦ ♦

MY FUTURE WOULD BE determined with the following letter and I had an idealistic vision. I was optimistic for a more promising destiny.

The phone rang. "Hello?"

It was the familiar voice of Frau Bors, "Hello Parastu! I have good news for you," she said, "Your transcript has been accepted. I will explain it further tomorrow at school."

I hung up the phone. My feet started floating off the floor. I was flying. My inner strength could overcome all odds. I looked at the world with the eyes of a lover. All the doors of my mind were open to any challenges. The excitement for a new beginning was so significant, that I wanted to rebuild the entire house from scratch. The sense of being somebody was closer than ever and when twilight covered the town, I begged the night to drop me off at sunrise.

The following day, I came to our usual meeting room with an apple in hand that I'd grabbed before leaving the apartment. Frau Bors always advised, "Parastu, start your day with breakfast. But if you can't, at least have an apple."

I got comfortable in the chair, pulled out my notebook and pen from my backpack, and laid them on the table. The door opened, and Frau Bors entered dressed in something classic and sophisticated, like always. I got up from my seat to greet her, a cultural tribute to elders. We greeted one another with a few sentences about my brothers and her mother. An envelope sat on the other side of the table.

"Parastu, this is the letter," Frau Bors said, "Congratulations! They've accepted your twelve years of schooling as comparable with the ten years of schooling here."

I swallowed hard and sat back in the chair. A mixed feeling of joy and sorrow weathered me.

Frau Bors continued, "This means that you can do Ausbildung."

I didn't ask why I couldn't apply for university. Deep down, that was my focus, the ashes of my burned phoenix, which I dwelled upon but could not utter. My cry was voiceless within me. I'd accepted that it was a silly fantasy and impractical to go to university. When everyone around me decided on Ausbuildung as a career path, I could not explain that I wanted more. I'd already learned that less means more.

I inched forward and reached for the letter in front of me. Since I knew the letter's contents, I quickly looked it over and put it back on the table. I looked at Frau Bors, who was patiently waiting for my response.

I broke the silence circulating the room and said, "Thank you so much, Frau Bors, for your effort."

I told her about the bakery's part-time job offer as well as the Ausbildung. She listened with keen eyes.

"Parastu, are you fond of baking? Working part-time is completely different than being a baker. There are so many other options that you can choose from."

I've never had much interest in being a chef, or studying baking. I was satisfied enough with daily meal preparation, nor did I want to spend lots of time in the kitchen.

"Can you make the Kolache Qaq[22]?" Aunt Razia had asked me the first year I'd arrived in Germany. Mom used to make the crisp cookies at home for every Eid celebration. It was her specialty. They expected me to be a master under Mom's supervision. Also, being an Afghan girl, it was a cultural notion that girls should be good in the kitchen. Girls being good in the kitchen was a promise for more suitors. Because of this, I was a huge disappointment. Instead, I yearned to be asked, "Parastu, read us one of your prose poems!" or, "Which books have you read?" or, "Introduce me to a new novel!"

"No, Frau Bors, I do not want to be a baker," I shook my head. "Back home, I wanted to become a doctor."

Frau Bors rested her hands on her thighs and leaned back. "Parastu, I know a dentist that is in search of a dental assistant. I could arrange a meeting with the dentist to find out more about the job and the schooling if you are interested?"

I knew little about dentistry. Back home, dentistry was not popular. There was the leading clinic located at the city center that I'd visited a couple of times with Mom. But I was not even familiar with the new technology. I did not know how to do an online search. Siawash got himself a computer, but I wasn't very

---

22 Salty, crispy cookies

curious. I also didn't want to break it since we couldn't afford to buy another one.

"Frau Bors, can you please explain a little about the dental assistant duties?" I asked.

She defined the responsibilities from her own experiences as a patient. "Parastu, it is best if you see it for yourself once we arrange a meeting," Frau Bors pointed out.

Without any further thinking, I said "Yes." My quick response could be attributed to my lifelong affair that I wanted to be somebody.

"Frau Bors, can you please make the appointment?" I pleaded earnestly.

Frau Bors and I both agreed on the dental assisting program, and we left with the agreement that she would set up an interview with the dentist.

Sunrise, the queen of enlightenment, woke me up to a bright dawn. The open window graciously scattered the brilliant rays of final spring days. I was greeted by the familiar habit of picking clothing for the interview, jeans and a button-up shirt. The only difference was the style of jeans which had wide legs. I wore my hair down, applied face cream and a soft pink lipstick.

Siawash was still sleeping, but I'd mentioned the interview with the dentist, which was around 9 a.m. Bliss satisfied my appetite for breakfast. I was full. I left the apartment with complete composure. The sky, the sun, the chirping birds on the trees, all stood at attention. I blew a kiss with a silent hello and walked to Frau Bors, who was waiting in her car.

"Good morning, Frau Bors," I said, followed with a smile.

"Morning, Parastu, how are you?"

"I am good. It's a beautiful day." I tried to keep her mind off breakfast, since I didn't want to lie to her. I knew she'd ask if I ate anything.

We drove fifteen minutes before she parked in the middle of the city center, near Hauptstraße.

We entered the office and stopped by the reception. The only receptionist behind the counter was dressed all in white, with short, blond hair.

"Good morning," she said.

Frau Bors mentioned our appointment with the dentist. A few minutes later, a man in his thirties appeared. He had a buzzcut and was almost my height. He dressed in a white shirt and pants.

"Hello, I'm Karl Olk," he introduced himself and went for a handshake.

"I'm Christine Bors," she said, and shook his hand.

"Parastu Ahang," I said, leaning forward to shake his hand.

Frau Bors taught me that a handshake can reveal much about someone's character. So I should always shake hands with a firm grip. He invited us to follow him to his office and have a seat.

We followed him into his office and sat in front of his desk. Frau Bors started talking first, introducing me, and ended by emphasizing my longing to study dental assisting.

He smiled. "Do you have any experience as a dental assistant? Do you know the duties?"

"No, I do not have any experience in this field," I explained, "But back home, I'd always wanted to become a doctor." I sat up straight, reaching for the right words to show my understanding of the language. "I was in the second year of university, my grade twelve being accepted as an equivalent to grade ten," I said, and presented the school board letter along with a handwritten resume.

"I am in search of another dental assistant to join my team," Dr. Olk explained, "The Ausbildung requires three days of practicum and two days of schooling. Parastu, when can you start?"

I had to stop my feet from skipping. My beaming gaze landed on Frau Bors.

"We have to apply for Ausbildung and find out when school starts," Frau Bors explained.

My inner sunshine roared and I added, "I am available now and can start even before school."

We got up and shook hands and I thanked him for his time and support.

In the car, we looked at each other.

"I did not expect this," I said, "I am touched and proud of the trust and belief Dr. Olk showed. I'm looking forward to starting school and working there."

We filled out the application and I interviewed with the school director of the dental assisting program. A couple of weeks later, I received a letter that I was enrolled in the three-years program. The study permit danced between my fingers and pride sped through my skin, my bones, and my veins.

I am not just a name. I have a career. I will free myself from my ugly circumstances. From now on, I will stand on my own two feet.

⁌⁍

In summer of 1991, I started the program. I entered the clinic and said hello to the receptionist. The other dental assistants came out and introduced themselves to me.

They welcomed me to the office and showed me around. I left my purse in the locker and hung my jacket onto the mounted wall hanger. We left the kitchen, passed the reception, and walked into every single room while she explained. The clinic was a decent size and very well put together.

When we walked into the lab she asked, "What size do you take for lab coat?"

"Small," I answered.

She handed me a white lab coat and continued, "You can wear this for the time being, until you get your uniform. Dr. Olk will pay for your order."

I left for the washroom to put on the white lab coat. I just wanted a few minutes alone with the coat. I embraced it, brought it to my nostril and breathed into it. Then I put it on, faced the mirror, and stepped out.

Days passed, and I got used to the environment. I went to school for two days and made friends with one of my classmates. We often worked on homework together.

I received my uniform; white scrubs. I asked Frau Schultz, "Can you mend pants?"

"Of course," she said, "I am so happy for you Parastu, for going to school."

Siawash and Arash were very proud of my progress, as well as Mom and Dad.

A few months into the program, I finished a long day of practicum and bussed home. I opened a frozen pizza and put it in the oven, then called Siawash for dinner. Zeal danced through my veins as I narrated my day.

"Today, I assisted Dr. Olk with fillings," I explained. "I seated the patient, draped her with an apron, and chatted with her while Dr. Olk was helping another patient." Siawash was quiet. I didn't wait for an answer. "I think I am getting good at this."

Siawash nodded his head and started washing the dishes while I made tea for myself. It was a rule in our home in Germany, whoever prepared the meal should not wash the dishes.

I turned the kitchen light off and carried my tea to the living room, dropping into the sofa chair facing the window. Siawash lay down on the couch, playing with an envelope in his hand.

"How was your day?" I asked, "You didn't say anything and you look tired. Are you okay?" He sat upright and handed me the envelope, already opened.

I glanced at him then grabbed the envelope. The top left corner showed it was from the Immigration and Refugee office. My fingers quivered and fished out the letter. I saw my name and address.

We regret to inform you that. . .

I avoided eye contact with Siawash and threw the letter on the table, knocking the tea cup on the floor.

The information on that paper was the murderer of the life I'd hoped for. The ruling once again confirmed my statelessness. If the mailman knew that what he was delivering would change everything I longed for, would he have delivered it? I asked myself.

I saw myself sitting on the couch as if from a distance. The evening gloom circled with silence. Twilight deepened my discontent as it wrapped its arm around me. I screamed inside.

What next? Am I going to be deported? What happens to my parents upon my return?

Belief. Confidence. Ambition. Faith. All these fancy words struck me with ridicule.

"Hamshira Jaan," Siawash spoke for the first time that evening, "I'm sure you will be granted another chance to apply for landed immigrant."

I said nothing. The tears could not stay quietly inside me any longer. They ran down my face my neck. I did not even bother wiping them away.

The following day, before starting work, I knocked at Dr. Olk's door. "Can I talk to you?" I asked.

"Of course, have a seat."

I explained my status and the letter I'd received.

"Parastu, this does not change anything," Dr. Olk said, "You can practice and continue going to school."

I did continue.

٭٭

THE YEAR 1991 SPUN on and new developments arose before me. Jebran, our family friend from Canada, proposed to me. Jebran was twelve years old when his father was imprisoned by the Government of Khalq and Parchm and sixteen years old when he arrived in Germany. Like many other Afghan refugees, he left amidst the upheaval and military recruitments in Afghanistan in search of harmony and a better life.

Jebran finished grade twelve in Germany and entered the auto mechanic program. After his family fled Afghanistan, they'd immigrated to Canada and a couple of years later, Jebran joined his family there.

We'd spoken several times and his family called my parents in Kabul, asking for my hand. We were all on different continents but within the same hemisphere. In the late stages of my maturity, autumn arrived. I did some soul-searching and considered Jebran to be a loving, gentle, young man and accepted his proposal. By the end of the year, Jeb came to Germany and we tied the knot before friends and family. After three weeks, he left to apply for my sponsorship.

At the start of 1992, the author of my destiny took a pen to a blank page to create a new plot and setting for my life and I surrendered.

Several months later, the postman dropped a letter with the Canadian Embassy address on it. The contents revealed my new home, and I was a Canadian landed immigrant. It was time to slowly announce my departure.

Since December of 1988, the word *goodbye* left me with scars. Any time I utter it, loneliness screams in my brain and tears comes without warning. Once again, I had to separate myself from my brothers, my family, and my friends. If I had the power, I would erase goodbye from the face of history.

                                          ⁘

FRAU BORS AND I visited a coffee shop on a damp but fresh afternoon. We'd passed many seasons together. It was the beginning of nature's rebirth. The ambiance of a restaurant was of great significance to Frau Bors. The eatery towered above the city, and the shop's tender vibe reminded our souls of gratitude. We settled in and were served coffee and cake.

After the regular conversation, Frau Bors asked, "Parastu, who is paying for your ticket?"

"I am." I had some money saved since I'd created a habit of saving from a young age.

"No, you are not. I will pay for your ticket," she said, "Parastu, I want you to have your own money with you. Be strong and independent, and call me if you need anything."

Dr. Olk wrote me a reference letter. Frau Shultz arranged a farewell party among our neighbors on the last Sunday afternoon before I departed. At 2 p.m., I rang her doorbell. There were five women, including myself, all of different ages. I was the youngest. The dining table was dressed in a white lace cover, and a porcelain rose coffee set decorated the surface. Home-baked cookies and cakes lay in the middle. At the center was the Frankfurter Kranz cake adorned with cream and cherries, sitting on a glass stand. Frau Schultz knew I loved Frankfurter Kranz. The aroma of fresh-brewed coffee filled the room as we chatted about the time we'd spent together.

"Parastu, it was a pleasure to get to know you. We all wish you a beautiful life together with your husband." She handed me a wrapped gift with a card signed by all my neighbors. Frau Schultz added, "Parastu, we got you a gift to be easy to travel with. It's something to remind you of us every day." She embraced me with her beautiful smile. It was a set of white towels.

"I'm so grateful for your kindness. I will never forget you all." It was time to say goodbye. Tears streamed from the overflow of my emotions and I hugged them all.

⁕

MY TICKET WAS PURCHASED, a foreign passport issued, and my bags were packed as I stood by the door of the room where I'd lived for the past three years.

Daybreak devoured the darkness. The dawn shouldered me through the sorrow. I escaped to the kitchen to prepare breakfast one last time for Arash, Siawash and myself.

We all waited for Frau Bors and Aunt Razia to arrive. The doorbell rang and I knew it was them. Arash and Siawash carried my luggage to her car. I grabbed my purse, wanting to be alone for a few minutes with the apartment that had witnessed so much sorrow and joy. Then I locked the door. I passed Frau Schultz's door, paused for a few seconds, and then I kept walking.

I took the stairs and with each story, I said goodbye. I opened the entrance door, saluting my home goodbye. I walked to the car. It was a regular day for everyone else. Nature was blooming into spring. It warmed my frigid body, filled my battered heart. A brisk wind whipped through half-naked trees, brushing my hair and whispering, *Parastu wherever you go, I am all around you.*

"Parastu, do you have everything, your passport and ticket?" Frau Bors asked.

"Yes, I have everything."

We drove to Dusseldorf airport. Passengers rushed all around me, heading to different places. I just wanted to ask them, are you going or coming home? Are you also a war survivor? We arrived early and it was not busy, so Frau Bors, Siawash, Arash, and Auntie accompanied me to the gate.

As I made my way through the exit at the Dusseldorf airport, I heard my own voice reciting the prose poem I'd written.

"Parastu?"

It's first grade, and my name resonates through the room. I am curious to know what my name means. I asked my father, "Can you please define Parastu?" My father collected himself and said, "A Parastu is a bird that conveys the longing of spring. In a distant time, when the cold weather is replaced by warmth, Parastus start appearing on the horizon to fly back home. Men, once they located Parastus, started celebrating the beginning of spring."

It's been years since Parastu left home from the ferocious winter. And still she flies from region to region, trying to call it home and return with the spring.

Where is Parastu's home? Who is Parastu?

It was time to say the ugliest word in the world, goodbye. I hugged and kissed each one of them, choked by my own tears.

No, I could not pronounce it. I could not say that offensive word.

"I love you," I said, and over and over I hugged them. I pulled Siawash and Arash into my arms. "I love you. I will get you to Canada. I will, and we will all be together again, I promise you. Arash, please take care of Siawash."

Auntie and Frau Bors rubbed my back and said, "Parastu, time to leave."

From that point on, I walked alone. I looked back and studied each one of them for the last time. I waved the final goodbye, and resumed walking towards the gate.

As soon as the plane took off, I could hold it together no longer and set my teardrops free. I wept for a long time. The aircraft traveled as fast as my beating heart, taking me to my new destination.

Eventually, I wiped my face and looked to see who sat beside me. At my right side was a lady who'd seen me sobbing. She greeted me with a warm smile.

"I am Lisa," she introduced herself in German, "I'm from Canada."

"I am Parastu. I'm joining my husband in Canada." The pilot announced that we were ready to land.

The plane touched the ground and I pushed out of my seat. I walked out with Lisa and we hugged each other.

"Best of luck with your future," she said, and handed me her address and phone number. "If you want a Canadian friend, I can be the one."

I grabbed her hand and held it in mine. "I would be honored and I will write to you."

I started walking towards a door with a sign that read:

WELCOME TO EDMONTON, CANADA.

I looked at the sign and said to myself, "Welcome to your new home and your ongoing quest."

Family Photographs

10 YEARS OF *age*

Kabul, Afghanistan

14 YEARS OF *age*

Kabul, Afghanistan

My parents in Kabul, Afghanistan, 1990

Frau Bors and me in Viersen, Germany, 1990

Jeb (my husband) and me in Germany, 1991

Chapter Eight

Someone was sleeping beside me. A man. My head spun. My eyes fixated on the ceiling. I lay on a double bed, the pink sunrise seeped through the window, mirroring the rosy, satin comforter.

I was married. I was in Canada. I have a hyphenated last name. I repeated these facts while I clung to the quilt.

Yesterday, the plane had landed in Edmonton. I went to the washroom and made sure I looked okay since I was someone's bride now.

After getting my luggage, I passed through Immigration and walked through an automated double door, which led me outside.

I had on a red and black jacket, a red skirt with black nylons and matching red and black flats. A black, velvet headband crowned my hair to keep it out of my face.

I pushed the trolley filled with my belongings. The automated door opened, and I saw a group of people standing around my husband. Jeb launched his way through his family, all of whom came to celebrate my arrival.

We hugged, our shoulders touching as his dark brown eyes landed on mine. We shied away from kissing out of cultural respect for others and my own timidity.

Jebran pressed his head to my ear and whispered, "Welcome to Canada, sweetheart," before handing me a bouquet of red roses. One by one, each person stepped forward, kissing me three times on each cheek, and then we drove to my in-law's house.

Late in the afternoon, my in-law's drove Jeb and me to our new, shared apartment in downtown Edmonton.

It is a cultural custom that the groom's family, and some of the bride's, drive the couple on their wedding night to their new home. In the olden days, weddings followed so many rituals and traditions. A vehicle would be adorned with flowers and at the end of the marriage celebration, the bride and groom would drive around the city. When the bride and groom arrived at their home, live music would welcome them, followed by friends and family dancing. Depending on the groom's wealth, a sheep or chicken would be butchered before them to signify prosperity. Women would accompany the bride to the kitchen to put her hand on the Halva, a sweet cooked before their arrival as a welcome to her husband's home.

⚓

THE APRIL AFTERNOON DISPLAYED a moderate, sunny temperature. But my brain could not spare any interest since my thoughts pulled me in other directions.

Siawash. What was he doing alone? Did he eat the food I left in the fridge for him? Arash left for university. Has he arrived safely?

Mom and Dad, how are they doing? I'm married. What does it mean? I carry someone else's last name, share a bed. It's no longer just me. It's we.

I stayed still in bed while yesterday's memory faded. I looked towards Jeb who was fast asleep.

Water. A sudden thirst for water waved into my body. I wondered whether I'd been a fish in a different life since water's freedom, its attitude, and its wild beauty had anchored my soul for eternity.

I poured myself a glass of water from the kitchen sink and went to the living room. The room was medium in size with sliding windows from wall to wall. I was surprised to see no door between the kitchen, dining room, and living room. The love seat leaned on the wall beside the kitchen. A TV with a video cassette recorder stood in the corner by a window, drawing my attention.

The TV started telling stories of the past. In Germany, Siawash and I decided to buy our own VCR. We cut back on groceries to save for a VCR. One afternoon, we visited a secondhand shop and paid one hundred marks for a VCR without a remote. Next, we rented a movie and Siawash, with his brilliant mind, used a broomstick as a substitute for the remote. Each moment of that night became a pleasant memory as we began our very first purchase and then created fun with simplicity.

In Kabul, Afghanistan, my dad purchased two TVs, a color one for the family room upstairs, and a black and white one for the living room downstairs. Every night for two hours, a program was broadcasted. It was something new, and not everyone in the neighborhood owned one.

My father opened the door of our house to all the neighbors and invited them to enjoy the program. The living room was L-shaped with a dining room attached. The black and white television sat on a wooden TV station at the front of the living room. Across from the TV at the back of the room was a traditional cherry-colored cuckoo clock; a little bird announced the approach of each hour. Men of all ages showed up to watch TV. They sat on the couches and floor. I hid in the corridor and listened to the men's laughter. Then, out of my curiosity, I couldn't help but spy on them. Even though the upstairs TV with color entertained Grandma and Mother, I so wanted neighboring women and girls to show up. Thus, we all sat together with the men and boys and watched TV and laughed.

Growing up, we lived in a two-story house owned by my parents. They'd built it before their wedding, and after its completion, had their wedding ceremony there.

Back home, the living room was only used for guests. It was locked on regular days and opened once a week for cleaning. When I lived at home in the seventies and eighties, people in Kabul visited as they pleased, without prior appointments or phone calls. Family and friends just showed up. The secured living room was reserved for that purpose. My mother held the key, and I was told where it was kept if someone showed up and she was not home.

The other cultural tradition we had was to always serve guests with tea and homemade cookies and, if they arrived around lunch or dinner, they were invited to have food. Mom always had baked goitshe fil and Kolache Qaq, elephant ears and crispy cookies, ready and stored in a locked metal box. Arash and I sometimes conspired to steal cookies. Once, we broke the lock and asked Siawash to lookout for anyone coming into the dining room. My father asked for the key on TV nights and unlocked the living room door before the neighbor's arrival, and Arash served them water or tea.

Another absurd childhood memory that put a grin on my face was the ice delivery during the month of Ramadan. Arash and I were bringing ice to the neighbors who did not have a fridge, mainly to shops near our house, before breaking fast. One evening, I collected the ice bowl from the freezer and, charmed by the snowflakes on top of the ice, ran my tongue over the ice. The bowl of ice stuck like glue to my tongue. Mom freed me by holding the bowl under running water in the sink.

"Morning breeze and human nature," I heard Jeb from the bedroom singing. I played with the glass of water and the present bounced back before my eyes. The question of where to begin and what to do next flashed from every corner of my mind. The future was tapping at my subconscious, my brain racing.

Jeb and I set up the table for breakfast and honored the couple's duties on our first day as husband and wife in Canada. I poured myself a cup of black tea, added some sugar, then grabbed a piece of toast but left it untouched.

"I'm off this week," Jeb said, "I took the week off to be with you."

"That's nice. Any plans?"

"No, I don't know. Let's go to Mom's house today."

"I want to go out to learn the language fast," I suggested.

"That is good idea."

"What about if I get registered soon?"

"I will take you to register for English classes," he said.

I swallowed and continued, "I want to help get Siawash to Canada. He's too young to be alone."

"I know an agency. We can talk to them about Siawash and sponsor him through them." My eyes sparkled, and I was suddenly full of vigor.

♣ ♣

It was a twenty-minute drive to my in-laws' house.

"Jasper Avenue is the city's main street," Jeb explained as he drove.

I started comparing it to the main road in Germany, which was a vibrant place. Stores opened for business from morning to evening on weekdays with a robust charm around the city. Coffee shops were always full of seniors and parents enjoying their free time with a friend.

Karte Parwan, a city of Kabul, was overpopulated and always busy. The noise of the fruits and vegetable stands and the loud music from stores and restaurants were overwhelming. Cars and animals such as donkeys carried loads of items while stray dogs rushed through the streets.

Edmonton seemed too quiet for my liking. It felt like being at a music venue, listening to loud music, when someone suddenly turns off the music.

On the week Jeb was off, he took me to register for two English classes: conversational and ESL[23]. Both classes were downtown and the bus stop was only a block away from our apartment. The

---

23   English as a Second Language

ESL class required an entrance exam to determine my comprehension level of the language in grammar and speaking. I scored to the intermediate level.

Jeb and I also visited the agency office to sponsor Siawash. The organization agreed on sponsoring him and we filled out the application. Next, we applied for my social insurance number. I checked off the three things I had on my to-do list.

The first day of speaking class began on the second week after my arrival. In the afternoon, I got off the bus and walked to the building, climbing the stairs to the second floor. I was early. The class was empty. Two, then three, and then eight students filled the classroom. We all were from different countries with varying cultural backgrounds.

"Good afternoon everyone," the instructor said as he entered.

"Good afternoon," we all repeated.

In our culture, students rose to their feet when the teacher arrived in the classroom.

The captain of the class chorused in Pashto, the other language spoken in Afghanistan, "Olar side." *Stand up.* And after everyone rose, she would continue, "Keshinky." *Sit down.*

Germany and Canada followed the same customs, no standing up.

The instructor introduced himself, accompanied by warm greetings. Then he asked us, "I would like each one of you to introduce yourself and tell us your future plans."

I sat in the middle. In the front row, a woman in her forties stood up and began her introduction. I could not hear a thing. My mind was busy preparing for my introduction. I practiced in my head. *My name is Parastu Ahang Mehdawi. I am from Kabul, Afghanistan, and my goal is to go to university.*

"Hahaha, nice try," I imagined the entire class breaking into laughter. "With the little English you have? You're a married woman. Hahaha, university nice joke!"

"Thank you, next," I heard the teacher say and as he looked at me. I got up and introduced myself.

"I want to have a career, " I said, and sat back down. The voiceless dream screamed inside me. I wanted a university degree, and more, but it seemed no one heard me.

I finished the ESL class and headed home but to my surprise, I saw Jeb waiting in the car to pick me up.

"Salam, Pari Jaan." It was the nickname he picked for me. In Farsi-Dari, Pari means fairy.

"Salam, honey. What are you doing here?" I asked.

"I finished work early. Mom phoned to have dinner with them. We're going to their house."

Everyone was quiet at dinner. Then tea was served and my mother-in-law pushed her way to me, reaching for my hand.

"My daughter," she cried.

A chill rushed through my spine and my body went limp as I dragged my hand out of hers.

"Is everything okay, Magul Jaan?" I asked, using the nickname for my mother-in-law.

She embraced me and said, "I am so sorry. Your grandma Bebe Kalan passed away. We just received a telegram from your dad."

Silence descended.

"I want to go home," I looked at Jeb and got up. I just wanted to be alone, to honor my Bebe Kalan's memory. Bebe Kalan was in her sixties, short with a slim build and gentle face. She had long white hair braided at the back of her head. She was always tidy and clean, wearing traditional white pants, a scarf, and a knee-length dress made of cotton and a light sweater. Bebe Kalan was constantly ill. She had angina, and most of the time, she was resting. Mom brought Bebe Kalan to stay with us after Sahar's family left the country.

I howled in solitude, remembering her wish, "Perwin Jaan, when I die, make sure to make a big, public announcement on the radio by mentioning all my children and grandchildren's names."

I called home, but there was no connection. I spoke with Auntie Razia. Arash and Siawash were as shocked as I was. Bebe Kalan had passed away from a massive heart attack on a day the city of Kabul experienced a killing spree by both sides, Mujahideen and the government.

Mom and Dad did not know what to do or how to bury her. They voted to put her to rest in the front yard. Once the neighbours found out, they volunteered to help and said, "Even if a bullet falls from the sky, we will bury grandma in the nearest cemetery." I heard the entire story from my parents once the line was reconnected.

* *

WE RECEIVED A PHONE call from the agency who sponsored Siawash explaining that they needed a few documents to process the application. In the morning, I left the apartment to drop off the documents and then took the bus to speaking class. Before leaving, I checked the mailbox and found a letter addressed to me. It carried my social insurance number card.

Sunday morning at breakfast, I said to Jeb, "Let's go to a shopping center. I really want to see what is inside all these malls."

Vaguely, I desired to see what was in style and fashionable plus to enjoy a day with my hubby.

His smile grew brighter. "Edmonton has one of the largest malls in the country. I will take you there."

The ride from our apartment to West Edmonton mall was about twenty minutes.

To my astonishment, it was something very new. I had never seen this type of shopping center, neither in Kabul nor in Viersen.

We started walking around. The different stores of clothing, jewelry, footwear, lingerie, and assorted businesses all under one roof amazed me. I wondered how big this shopping center could be.

We proceeded to cruise and found ourselves in front of an indoor water park and swimming pool. It was gigantic. With wide eyes we looked at the waterpark. So many people were at the pool, enjoying their Sunday afternoon with family and friends.

Eventually, we got hungry, and it was almost the middle of the day, so we decided to have lunch. Jeb suggested a food court which was another new experience for me. I accepted with delight, and we walked there. It was an enormous area with all different fast-food stores. I loved the idea that anything you could think of was all gathered under one roof. Anyone could easily spend a full day of amusement and fun there. We each got our favorite food from different fast-food places and found an empty table to sit at.

My brain targeted a new scheme. The notion of working at the most impressive shopping center in the country planted itself in the garden of my soul.

"What if I applied for work in one of these clothing stores?"

"How would you get here?" he asked, "I guess if you worked only on the weekends, I could drive you back and forth."

"I'll go inside a store and ask if anyone's hiring. I've dressed appropriately for job hunting, and there's no need to postpone it."

He agreed. I entered a couple of stores for the purpose of employment. Some salesclerks gave me an application to fill out, and some said they weren't hiring. Jeb helped me fill out some applications, and I quickly returned them to the salesclerks. We spent most of the day of as a couple in the plaza.

One afternoon, after the transcendent weekend at the mall, the phone rang.

"Hello?" I answered.

"Can I talk to Parastu?" a female voice asked.

"Speaking," I responded.

She introduced herself as the manager of the Mariposa clothing store at the West Edmonton Mall.

"Can you come in for an interview on Saturday at 11 a.m.?"

"Yes!" I said without thinking. And in my mind, I repeated, yes, yes, yes!

I started my first job in Canada two months after my arrival, at Mariposa, inside one of the largest malls in the country.

Chapter Nine

I was fourteen years old in grade ten. Before schools reopened after winter break, I demanded to purchase a new pair of shoes. Thus, I saved my allowance and the celebratory money that I'd received from my parents and family. During the Nowruz and Eid festivities, part of the cultural ceremonies is that children and young adults were given money by elders as a token. So, Mom and I decided to go shopping and make it a fun day by eating out.

The shopping bazaar that we wanted to go to was called the American Plaza, or Sarye Americayee, located in Deh-Afghanan[24]. It was one of the famous bazaars, the clothes and garments imported from abroad. The prices were affordable. The business hours were seven days a week, from eight in the morning until sunset.

Deh-Afghanan is in the center of Kabul and hugged by restaurants, bus stations, markets, hotels, fruit stands, and retail kiosks. Many kebab restaurants sit beside one another on the same street. In opposition, they employed a young or middle-aged man as a front man to promote the business.

---

24 Central city in Kabul

We left home for the bus stop down the street. Our house was on a steep road and near the Asamai mountain. It was about a twenty-minute walk to get to the bus stop. I packed my small black clasp bag with the saved money and draped it over my shoulder. We arrived at the bus stop. There were no bus schedules, but we knew it ran every hour.

The buses were always highly crowded, but there were no structures set. So, individuals would charge towards the bus to be one of the lucky few to make it inside.

Women climbed aboard from the front door and men from the back. We got in and stayed with other women and children. The men were all at the rear of the bus. The seats were all occupied by elders. Everyone else was standing, either holding onto the handrails or held at the mercy of the crowd. Mom and I got separated inside the bus. The Killiner, a title for the fare collector, a young man in his mid-twenties, pushed his way through to accept money. Mom paid for both of us. The bus stopped at different locations, people got in and off the bus with the same routine. Finally, we arrived at the central station of Deh-Afghanan. We hurried out since no one had the patience to wait. Someone shoved me down, and I landed on the street.

Mom and I started walking to Saraye-Americayee. It was another ten minute walk to get there. We passed a few small fruit stands and other shops and finally reached our destination.

Saraye-Americayee was always packed. The distance between the stores on the left and right was so small, only two people could walk side by side. The open-air bazaar was filled so full with clothing hanging outside, we could hardly see the sky.

We passed a few clothing stores, but a shoe shop at the very end of the row drew our attention.

A middle-aged man yelled with an upbeat voice, "Sister, welcome to my store. We have all kinds of shoes for men, women and children. Good price! Made for you!" he chanted at a tongue-twisting speed. These types of jobs were always held strictly by men.

"Salam, brother," Mom said as we followed him inside the store.

"Salam, sister," said the salesman.

I looked around. A pair of black, leather ballet shoes caught my eyes. I tried them and they were just my size. They were also really comfortable and would be perfect for school.

"How much are they, Uncle?" I asked.

"For you, they are free," he smiled. "They are cheap." He mentioned the price.

"No, brother, these are expensive," Mom said. Then she explained, "She is a student. She saved her money, give her a good discount."

The shoe keeper answered, "No, sister, I can't. I make no profit. I already gave you a good price."

My eyes flew from Mom to the salesman, in hopes she would conquer. I fixed my mind on those shoes, and while they bargained I walked around the store.

"Brother, is that your last price?" Mom asked.

"Yes. I cannot lower it anymore. I make no money on it."

Mom looked at me and said, "Take them off. We'll go to the next store. There are lots of other stores. This is really expensive."

I took the shoes off and carried them back to the shoe rack. One finger at a time, I let go of the shoe while avoiding eye contact with both Mom and the salesman.

We were almost on the next road when he screamed, "Come on sister, get your shoes." His voice entered my ears like a melody. Mom and I turned around and walked back to the store.

I approached the merchant to pay. The retailer did not own a cash register. Instead, he carried cash in his pockets. He had on traditional clothing called Piran Tunban, or a dress and trousers.

Clack. I unlocked the clasp purse, and my jaw dropped. The black fabric inside the bag was naked and empty.

"Mom, Mom! Someone stole my money."

She looked at me and said, "No worries, I will pay for it. But always be sure to keep your purse under your arms."

"Kebab, delicious kebab! Chapli kebab! Come on sister, seats are available at the back." A young man stood in front of the restaurant, summoning us to dine in. I took small bites of the spicy Chapli kebab, one of my favorites, as my brain tried to investigate the robbery.

＊＊

"HONEY, HAVE A GREAT day at work. I will pick you up five," Jeb said.

I blinked back to the present.

I kissed him. "Thanks, honey. Say hi to Magul Jann. See you later."

The front store was closed. It was 9:45, so I knocked. A coworker opened the door and guided me to the back to the manager. The store was big, with the cash register a few steps from the front door. The changing room was at the very back along with a small staff.

The morning began with introductions, signing papers, the going over the week's schedule and job training. My shifts during weekdays were from 5–9 p.m. twice a week, and a complete day shift on the weekend.

I was studying new vocabulary at school, and in the evening and weekends, I used them by having small conversations with customers. At the end of summer, winter shipments arrived and the manager held a meeting to introduce the new products. The following Sunday, I took my position at the middle of the store.

I walked around and tidied up the racks when a mother and daughter entered the store. I approached them with a smile, using every tool of customer service I had.

"Good morning. Are you looking for any particular items?" I asked, "Can I help you with anything?"

"Yes," the mother answered, "We are looking for a winter jacket for my daughter."

Pride crowned my head as I thought of how I could put all my abilities to the test.

"Please follow me," I said, and escorted them to where the newly arrived jackets were displayed. "We got these jackets last week." I pointed to the coats, "It is a lined parka, comes in two different colours, black and white. Good quality, and it does not shrink."

I repeated the word in my mind. *Shrink, past tense, shrank.* I continued, "May I ask for your size?"

They loved the jacket and bought the white one. I succumbed to vanity and strived to learn more vocabulary.

BACK HOME IN KABUL, I wrote a prose poem by the name of Phoenix, or Qoqnos. In my teenage years, I started being interested in writing, especially in prose poetry. My father regarded this subject with a very high value. So, he encouraged me with more books from famous Farsi- Dari poets and authors such as Mohammad Hejazi, Sadegh Hedayat, and Jamal Zadeh[25]. Naturally, I regarded Hejazi's style with admiration.

Father also introduced me to Western literature and authors such as Leo Tolstoy and Maxim Gorky. My love for poetry influenced me to commit to memory any verse or prose that I really cherished.

La Lac, or *The Lake*, one of Lamartine's famous poems, I memorized. On the following day, Gulali, after finishing her chores, came upstairs to do her last inspection. I asked her if she could listen to the poem that I'd studied by heart. Gulali lay down on the mattress while I traveled up and down the family room, reciting the poem. After I was done, I turned around and saw that Gulali was fast asleep.

Father presented me with books on different movements, styles, and devices of literature. I was drawn to the surrealism artistry form; an idealistic approach was more attractive than reality. Father emphasized realism rather than imagery, and he encouraged me to try the writing style of the new era, realism.

One of my father's friends was a poet and was famous for his writing in society. Father asked him if he could educate me on prose poems, and he agreed. His name was Ayena, meaning Mirror. He visited Dad at least twice a week and he set one visit

---

25   All three are Iranian writers

aside to guide me by teaching me the principles of creative writing. Father was also present in the room when he was teaching me, not that my father could not trust him, but there was no need for him to leave. He reckoned I was a shy girl.

On one of his regular routine visits, Friday afternoon, I heard my name called after they'd spent half an hour catching up on the daily news and politics. I happily grabbed my notebook and ran from my room to the living room.

"Salam Uncle," I said and kissed his hand. I took a seat in front of him and my father. He delivered my last essays back with some notes on them.

"Your next homework is about a bird called Qoqnoos, or phoenix." He narrated the mythology of the phoenix and continued, "Let me see what you can do about this bird, surprise me."

I got up, said goodbye, and left the room with the phoenix in my head. The Qoqnoos spoke to my subconscious. I wondered, what could it be? The night undressed into pink and orange. In my mind, I saw a baby phoenix flying upon the blended shades. It spread its wing and flew higher and higher until I could no longer see it. I smiled and fell asleep.

The following week when Uncle Ayena came back to see my father, I presented the essay. The essay was titled, *Fire and Ashes* and read:

"The phoenix is a bird that lives for a long time. On the last day of her existence, she is not quiet. When twilight drops its black curtain on the face of the horizon and the stars twinkle around the moon when the shadow of illusion and fear hugs the town when the nocturnal birds honour the dusk. The phoenix starts singing in distress. Her voice deepens as the sky changes to an orange-pink colour, and she becomes louder and louder. Alas, amid the unrest, the phoenix gets into a blaze and burns to the ground. Dawn advances with the sun climbing on the shoulder of the cliff, and a young phoenix is born from her mother's ashes and soars to a new adventure. This is the fate of the phoenix.

"What is it? Do I see a parallel between this story and a human's path through life? I wonder, as long as mankind sees Mother Earth dress and undress into spring, summer, fall, and winter. Until we taste the nectar of life and smell the scent of an annual cycle. As long as we hear the birds' chorus among the trees, our hearts desire and transcend for a lover's touch. And such is the destiny of mankind."

"I really like the metaphor," he said, "I agree that human longing has no end and the human soul in the mystery of creation, is fascinated by any beauty. Well done."

I looked at Father.

"Bravo, my daughter."

⁂

"HONEY, I WANT TO learn how to drive, "I said to Jeb one day. Jeb started phoning around to find a driving school for me to attend. The school I signed up for was three times a week of practice and two days of lessons. I finished the driving practice within a couple of months as well as the lessons.

"Can I take the road test?" I asked the instructor one day.

"I don't think you're ready," he said, "You need a few more lessons and also practice with your husband."

"I'm sorry, I think I am ready. I want to give it a try," I insisted.

The following week, the teacher drove me to the exam area. I was nervous and nauseated, but nothing could stop me from my quest.

The road test examiner pulled the paper from the clipboard with a red circle stating I'd failed.

"You passed everything else, but failed at parallel parking," the driving tutor explained.

The instructor dropped me off by our apartment. The elevator opened, and I heard the phone ring from our apartment. I rushed to open the door.

"Hello?" I answered.

"Mrs. Mehdawi, can we book an appointment for you and your husband to come in? We have some news from the Immigration and Refugee office."

"I can come tomorrow."

"Eleven in the morning," he said.

Jeb could not miss work, but I did not want to wait. I was eager to know how soon I could have my baby brother by my side.

"I am sorry, Mrs. Mehdawi. Your sponsorship has been denied since your brother lives in a safe country," the gentlemen from the agency said and presented me with the letter.

I grabbed the letter and left. Memories of Siawash, tears, and I walked back home together. I skipped both English classes, just traveled to the three years Siawash and I'd spent together. Moments, hours of each day, performed in my mind. *He is not even eighteen years old yet, why did I leave without him? There must be some other way to sponsor him.* I tortured my thoughts until I fell asleep.

＊＊

IN THE SAME MONTH, I signed up for the second road test. The idea of what others might think if I failed a second time was debilitating. I tried everything to master it. I took a couple more lessons with the teacher. Jeb owned a manual car, so I could not use it, but he showed me how to parallel park.

The test was at nine in the morning, but I woke up at seven. I was so nauseous and I vomited a couple of times. I made myself breakfast, but just the smell of food made me throw up.

＊＊

"YOU LOOK PALE," THE instructor said, then continued, "Don't worry, you are ready this time." He smiled, "You will only be tested on parallel parking."

I tipped my head back and held my hand over the mouth to keep from gagging. I took the test and passed.

I wrote to my Canadian friend. *Dear Lisa, I try to adjust to this new chapter of my life, and I just got my driver's license!*

Lisa replied, *Parastu you are officially self-reliant, congrats*!

We continued writing to one another for a while.

The following day, I could barely open my eyes. From head to toe I was in agony. Jeb was gone at work. I forced myself out of bed but canceled my evening shift and missed class. One block down the road was a walk-in clinic. I reasoned that it was best to get antibiotics. It was of utmost importance that I not miss any more classes or working shifts.

I seized whatever attire I could find, clothing my chilled yet hot body. Then I forced my legs towards the clinic. The receptionist received me and directed me to the waiting room.

"Mrs. Mehdawi," My name was called after waiting almost forty minutes. I got up and followed the assistant to the room.

"What brings you here?" she asked.

"I have fever and body aches," I answered.

After another ten minutes of waiting, the doctor finally walked in, introduced himself, and wanted to know the problem.

I explained my condition in detail this time. I wished this to be over soon so I could go back home and glue myself to my bed.

The doctor started to do the physical examination by checking my throat, ears, chest, and vital signs, and then he asked, "Are you pregnant?"

My body shivered more. I pushed with my palms on the medical exam table to control my balance.

"No," I answered, then repeated myself, this time with doubt, "No, no."

"Mrs. Mehdawi, please give a urine sample to rule the suspicion out," he said, and he left the room.

I set the container on the counter beside the washroom door and came back to the room. Underneath my skin, I could hear the flow of blood through my arteries and veins.

Pregnant? No, I am not. I just moved to this new land not even a year ago. I am a wanderer myself. I want to stand on my own feet. I want to go to school, have a career. No, I am not pregnant. I still have lots to learn.

My glance flew back to the table, the chair, the sink, back to me, round and round aimlessly. *Mother.* I love this title, I honor the definition of this title. I want my own mother to be with me. I surrendered, my eyes moistening

The door opened, and the doctor walked in with my chart in hand. His head turned towards me in slow motion, pausing for a second.

"Mrs. Mehdawi."

My whole body was in my ears, waiting to hear his answer.

"The result came back positive. You are pregnant."

I said nothing. Tears showered my face and kissed my cheeks.

Chapter Ten

"Parastu, you did not come for a few days. Were you sick? You missed out on so much. Go get your handouts from the instructor," the class mate whom I sat with said.

"Thanks I am better now. What did he say" I asked.

"He said if any of us want to continue to study further, we should sign up for night classes," she continued, "We should have grade ten, eleven, and twelve math and English. But it all depends on what career we want to pursue. I know you want to study more."

I bused home; my eyes could only see mothers with children on the bus. It felt like the universe was pregnant. I was whipped from overthinking. I have never been around infants or small kids. I know nothing about parenting. *How can I raise a child and go to school? How can I mother a child if I have not even fully developed myself? How I can I teach a child when I am still learning?*

The mental image of peoples' judgments drifted my focus. *She is going to school, how selfish, look at her life, she is failing both. You are married. You are going to be a mother. This is your identity.*

I covered my ears and ran to my parents' arms for comfort.

"Bebe Jaan, Bebe Jaan?" I said as I held the phone receiver with both hands.

"Hello," I heard Mom's voice on the other side of the phone and relaxed. I'd tried their number a couple of nights in the row and kept calling. "Hello?" It was Mom. The weight of her sound started me weeping, and tears gripped my throat.

"Bebe Jaan, Par—it is Parastu."

"Parastu Jaan, my daughter, nice to hear your voice, how are you? How is Jebran Jaan?"

"Bebe Jaan, Bebe Jaan, I am pregnant." Droplets soaked my face.

"My beautiful daughter, amazi—"

The line got disconnected. I wiped the tears from the phone receiver, and hung up.

Within twenty-four hours, Mom and Dad spent lots of money to send us a telegram that read: Parastu and Jebran Jaan, congratulations. We are lucky to be grandparents.

Next, I called Frau Bors and told her. Following that, I received a postcard from her congratulating me on my pregnancy.

Jeb glowed with joy, and he sang like a nonstop radio station, "We will be parents! I will be a father and Pari Jaan, you will be an amazing mother."

⁕⁖

Experiencing motherhood was so noble. The thought of someone growing inside me was precious. It was so big that I wanted to bow down and hug life for its virtue. A stream of energy flowed through my veins. I would be a mother.

I signed up for grade ten math and English at community college, which I could start the following semester. I continued working at Mariposa and resumed my morning English classes. I could not practice my driving. Jeb had a manual and we couldn't afford to sell the car and buy an automatic.

The first five months of pregnancy was a journey in vomit, fatigue, and sickness. My stomach started growing. My nose and face got all puffed up. I craved subway sandwiches and ordered them with extra hot chilli peppers. Mood swings followed me throughout the nine months. I cried witnessing the movement of a human being inside me, smiled at the awe-inspiring sensation of a tiny fist moving in my belly. It was simply poetry.

I visited the library to check out books on how to care for an infant. The other thing that helped me was connections with the coworkers and classmates. A few of them were parents. We did not have a close relationship outside work or the classroom, but we talked and I mostly asked questions just on our breaks. Reading books was an idea I picked from them.

I also learned that we could request to find out about our baby's gender. For both of us, having a healthy infant was the most essential thing. In our culture, having a boy was valued higher than girls. It is the cultural gender fondness. Remarks such as, "If you carry your baby low, it is a boy. If you like sweets, it is a girl. If labour pain is sharp, it is a boy," were common, but I did not pay any attention.

In May of 1993, at around one in the morning, a piercing pain woke me up. I went to the washroom and went back to bed. Traveling to the washroom became a distraction. I went to the living room and lay down on the couch. The on and off discomfort kept me on my feet. The city behind the window changed in color. The street, the trees, became visible. The cars on the road made noise to wake the town up. The daylight reckoned it was time. I woke up Jeb to take me to the hospital. While Jeb was registering, the nurse put me in a wheelchair and took me to the maternity ward.

She pushed me to a room that had only one bed facing the window and two portable tables beside the bed. Another nurse, who was already in the room, passed me a blue gown to put on. Both nurses helped me to get to the bed. One fixed the pillow and the other patted my hand.

"The doctor will be here soon, do you need anything else?"

I shook my head. The stroke of their kindness weaved into my vulnerable mind and body like a mother's caresses. The stream of tears stopped me from speaking.

Jeb dialed his mother's number to inform them of my condition. They all arrived shortly one by one, sitting in the waiting room.

The doctor appeared, accompanied by a few visitors, "Hello! It is time to welcome your baby to the world." Her presence was a therapeutic catharsis to my anxiety.

She read the chart and continued, "Let me introduce to you the Faculty of Medicine students, they will follow me around today. Is it okay with you if they observe the delivery?"

The white lab coats they wore waved hello and sent an acute anguish through me as I recalled my lost wish to attend university.

"Of course."

"Thanks. I will be back," the doctor said and left the room followed by the students. Tears followed as the door closed behind them, streaming upon my wounded heart.

Morning turned to late afternoon, and I was in the sway of excruciating pain. Magul Jaan, Jeb's mom, rubbed my back with her gentle hands to lessen the soreness. The throbbing pain compounded inside me, banishing any thoughts from my mind, even the desire for the presence of my mom.

The two nurses informed the doctor of my robust anguish and returned with a message.

"The doctor is suggesting an epidural for pain. She also thinks that she can induce the labor," they said.

"Is my baby in any danger?"

"Baby is fine. It's just to make the process faster for you," they explained.

I refused both suggestions.

It was around nine in the evening when I saw the doctor all dressed up in a gown and mask. A few students with same attire trickled in behind her. I noticed the entire atmosphere of the room changed. They asked my in-laws to wait in the waiting room. Jeb, at my request, stayed with me, and they asked him to scrub and wear the gown.

The doctor sat near the lower part of the bed and explained things to the students. Everyone in the room was doing their jobs and I did mine.

"Mrs. Mehdawi, push! We are almost there," the doctor demanded.

I was exhausted, and turned to Jeb with a forlorn glance.

Next, I heard the doctor say, "One more push! I see a head full of hair."

I roared with all I had left in my fragile and fatigued body.

At exactly twenty minutes past ten in the evening, "It's a boy! It's a boy! Mrs. Mehdawi, you mothered a son," I heard the doctor and the nurses yell.

The sun pushed its way to dawn as existence unraveled its mystery before my eyes. I felt warm. Eighteen hours of agonizing labor pain crowned me with a title. *Mother*. This title meant love, devotion, tenderness, respect, power, kindness, yearning, passion, and honor.

Tears, my only companion in every instant, poured down and danced all around me.

Jeb caressed my face in triumph and raced outside to his family.

◆◆

A PROMISE I MADE as a young girl surfaced when I became a mother. I would name my son Yuseuf and my daughter Saharr. When my Grandma Bobo Jaan came to sleep over at our house, we lay beside her and asked her tell us a story. One night she told us the story of Yuseuf the Prophet.

We named him Yuseuf.

I read more books from the library about parenthood. My meticulous personality wanted to be more than good. I did not want people to think less of me as a mother. I had an eastern mind in the western world.

One evening, after the usual bedtime routine, Jeb and I planned to have chicken fondue and watch a movie. Half an hour later we heard Yusuef crying. We tried to calm him down and resume our plan. His discomfort progressed. We tried everything we knew and called Magul Jaan for advice. We decided to take him to the clinic. We got in the car and, to our surprise, he fell asleep. We found ourselves driving around the town aimlessly just to let him rest.

The unfulfilled part of me for education still yearned for that path of possibilities. When Yuseuf turned six months old, I started picking up the pieces of myself again. I continued with the Math and English studies in the evening and finished the requirements for getting into a community college. A list of programs was handed out by the instructor. Accounting was on the top of the list. I remembered Father saying that accounting was the skeleton of any business. I applied for accounting. It was a one-year program, full-time, with five weeks of practicums that ran twice a year. I met the requirements and got accepted to the first round.

My impetuous personality put me on the same path over and over. I just wanted to feed my ego and be somebody. I encountered this problem in all three countries. In Kabul, the Faculty of Medicine was a vague promise. In Germany, the experience was a faint dream. And in Canada, I was like an orphan, growing up on my own.

IN THE YEAR OF 1994, on an early January morning when the month was still raw and cold, the doorbell rang. I pressed the intercom button.

"Who is it?"

"Mrs. Mehdawi, I have a telegram for you," a male voice said.

"I will be down in a minute," I answered.

I held Yuseuf in my arms and took the elevator to meet the mail man. He handed me a telegram from Mom and Dad.

It read: "Your father and I are going to your Aunt Sharifa's for winter."

My Aunt Sharifa, my father's sister, who lived in Peshawar, Pakistan and had escaped the war a year earlier. She was a refugee who awaited sponsorship from a western country where her children lived.

A flow of hysteria raced through my bloodstream, knowing my father would never leave his homeland. *What happened? Are they in any immediate danger? Were Arash and Siawash also in disbelief?*

Forty-eight hours of sleepless nights and overanalyzing passed with no news of my parents. Mid-afternoon of their third day missing, the phone rang. I jumped and picked up the phone.

"Parastu Jaan, my daughter," it was Mom.

I released a big breath, held back tears, and said, "Bebe Jaan where are you? Is Dad with you? What is going on?"

"We are in Peshawar. I am calling from a store that allows overseas phone calls. This is the number if you want to contact us. Just call to let them know the time and we will be informed." She continued, "It is a really bad winter back home but we are with your aunt. Your father is fine and we'll return after winter."

I didn't know why Dad lived in an illusion. Peace was only a fantasy.

Afghanistan was like a myth my grandma once told. "Once upon a time, a demon had occupied the village. It was dark everywhere, people were rushing to find harmony, and life melted in the hands of beasts."

I bled inside for innocent civilians.

I called Germany to let Arash and Siawash know Mom and Dad were okay and had arrived in Pakistan.

"Honey, I am worried about my Mom and Dad," I raised my concern to Jeb, "You and I know how bad the situation back home is, Mom could not voice it. They are afraid of spies, but Dad still believes democracy will prevail, and I know he does not want to be a burden to his children." I continued, "I am not going to let them go back to that war-torn country. War stole my youth, my dreams, and cut our family into pieces. I am not going to stand and watch that war separate me from my parents once again. Let's find a way to bring them here."

"Let's book an appointment with the immigration office and take it from there," he said.

This was my first priority, besides Yuseuf. Deferring my studies to September was the first objective on the checklist. My patriotic father would refuse the idea of leaving the Motherland for good, so I did not reveal my plot to them. We met the necessary terms, paid the application fees, and a couple of weeks later, we got a letter from the immigration office that they'd accepted our application and sent the request to the Canadian Embassy in Pakistan.

My racing mind could not fathom the concept of waiting. When I said goodbye at the Kabul Airport, I did not know whether it would be possible for my eyes to witness hellos. I announced that I want to go to Pakistan.

"Pari, you know that once the application gets approved, they will arrive soon," he said, "You know I work full time, I can only take care of Yuseuf during nights. My mom can help during the day."

"Knowing Dad, he may refuse the sponsorship. I want to convince him myself. I'll take Yuseuf with me." Nothing could stop me from going to Pakistan, nor did I want to part from my son.

"I support your decision," Jeb said.

We applied for passports and a visa to the Pakistan Embassy. I packed my bags, held my nine-month-old son in my arms, and with the sponsorship letter in hand, I flew to Pakistan.

It was a twenty-three hour flight to Islamabad, Pakistan with two stops in Toronto and Frankfurt, Germany. I took advantage of the situation and stayed overnight in Frankfurt to visit Arash and Siawash. I had not seen them for two years. During the course of two years, much had changed.

First, Arash was done with his studies and employed in a full-time position. Second, Siawash had transformed into a man. He was no longer the young boy. He was preparing for the university entrance exam. Third, I was a mother and introduced them to my new family.

Arash held Yuseuf in his arms for hours. We stayed up late that night. The following day they accompanied me to the Frankfurt airport and walked me to the gate. I hugged them with

Yuseuf in my arms. Tears poured down my face. Yuseuf played with the droplets in his tiny palm.

"I love you. I love you, Arash and Siawash."

After ten hours of cutting through beds of clouds the pilot announced, "Ladies and Gentlemen, we are landing at the Islamabad airport shortly. Please fasten your seat belts."

Bang! The plane touched the ground. My son and I had cruised over three continents, the Atlantic ocean, and the Aegean sea to visit my parents after six years.

My heart galloped and I suppressed a shiver, as I remembered a friend's advice before leaving for Pakistan.

"When the plane lands in Islamabad airport, make sure to wear a scarf to cover your head. Also, in order to make things easier, you should consider bribes."

Yuseuf's little legs hugged my waist. I placed one arm under his bottom and one hand to keep the headscarf from sliding. I followed the passengers to the baggage claim area, got my bags, and secured them on a cart. We arrived at the customer check-in area where a lengthy line had formed all the way to the end of the room. I stood behind an array of passengers as Yuseuf grew restless.

I wondered. *How can I bribe them? What do I say? Should I have the money ready in my palm and, if so, how much?*

Sweat soaked my skin, and I felt like Yuseuf might slide down to the floor. In my effort to keep him from sliding, a policeman stood up and pointed at the end of the line.

"Ma'am, come over here," he shouted.

I looked around to make sure he was not pointing at me. He was.

Why me? Was my scarf not satisfactory? Am I in any trouble?

My fight or flight triggered my nerves and I immediately thought of flight. I thought, *I'll ask him to please send me back to Canada.*

My trembling, sweaty feet carried me upfront. Gasping at the counter, Yuseuf and I arrived while I parked the baggage cart behind us.

The officer asked for my passport, and without further investigation, he stamped it and said, "Jaho." *Go.*

The sweat dried up immediately, and my body rushed with gratitude, "Thank you, thank you, thank you."

Heads and bodies rushed before my eyes in the arrivals terminal. The area was highly congested, with scarcely any leeway. I stepped forward looking for a familiar face. Yuseuf and I were squished between strangers. Ear-piercing screams of English, Pashtu, and Urdu circulated. Taxi drivers tried to sell their services by pulling on passengers' luggage.

My vision searched strangers' profiles for the comfort of a family member, and none came. Yuseuf roused, weeping, his little arms coiled around my neck. Guilt gnawed at me and I pushed his head on my face and cried.

"I am sorry, my baby. I am so sorry. I did not know I'd put you through chaos. My fault. . . I am sorry. I love you." Fear consumed me and I surrendered, freeing the other hand and hugging him with both arms.

"Parastu, Parastu, Parastu Jaan."

I lifted my face from his head. Was I imagining it or was someone really calling my name?

My eyes chased the sound and I saw a face with a white hair and beard, a head taller than the surrounding people. I pushed my way through like a cheetah to get to the arms of that white-bearded man. My heart hopped up and down. I threw myself into his arms.

"Padar Jaan, Padar Jaan." He was my father and, as when I was a child, all my worries dissipated.

Once Father saw his first grandson, his mind changed. He accepted leaving everything behind and immigrate to Canada. Mom and Dad could not go back home to claim their belongings due to the outbreak of battle. They sent a message to Gulali and her husband and made them the guardians of the house. The money they saved, including Dad's retirement, remained dormant in the bank.

In November of 1994, two months after I began the accounting program, my parents arrived in Edmonton, Canada. We moved to a bigger apartment to accommodate all five of us.

The arrival of my parents lifted an enormous weight of responsibilities off my shoulder. Beside full time school, I held a part-time job at a clothing store. Jeb worked full time as a manager in a restaurant which required long shifts. Yuseuf was growing up with my parents' whole love and attention. He started speaking Farsi-Dari and English words through his own creativity. He called me Boty, a name that did not exist in Farsi nor in English. It was only a name of tenderness between mother and son.

On an ordinary day the following year, everyone completed their daily tasks as usual. But it was a big day for me. I dressed up to attend the Canadian Citizenship Ceremony. I stood before a judge, took oaths, and listened to the rights and duties bestowed upon me. And by noon, I was a Canadian citizen.

Chapter Eleven

I finished my accounting program in Edmonton, Alberta, and started looking for jobs. I applied for anything in the accounting field, but I preferred a payroll officer position. In reality, deep down in my core, none of these careers stirred my emotions. I viewed them as my duties. I scanned newspapers, dropped off resumes, and made phone calls.

"Sorry, you don't have experience."

"We are looking for a more experienced individual."

"We will keep your resume on file."

These were the typical answers I received. I couldn't even reason with them by asking, "If you don't offer me a position, where will I gain the experience?"

I continued in retail and worked full time while applying for a volunteer role in accounting. Finally, Edmonton SPCA granted me an unpaid bookkeeping position.

On my first day at Edmonton SPCA, I was greeted by two rows of cages. As much as it hurt me to see those beautiful creatures locked in, they encouraged me to reciprocate their warm welcome with a big smile. Two memories ignited a bittersweetness in my soul.

"Parastu," Mom called. I was eight years old and it was a Friday. Sahar and I played hopscotch on the front yard balcony.

"Coming," I yelled back. Sahar and I ran to the kitchen where Mom was.

"Take this to Auntie Kamela." Mom handed me a serving bowl to take to our next-door neighbor.

"What is it Bebe Jaan?"

"Mastawa[26]. I made it for lunch."

"Oh no, I don't like it. Can I eat French fries?" I asked.

"Try it. This is different than Shola," Mom said. They were both special Afghan dishes.

I held the bowl with both hands, accompanied by Sahar. Sahar knocked on the door, and Auntie Kamela opened the door.

Woof, woof! A big head jumped underneath her arms and reached for the bowl. The dish landed on the ground as Sahar and I turned and ran. The dog caught me by the leg, and since I couldn't move, he bit me.

In Germany, I met a mother and daughter on a train. The three of us got to know one another and we exchanged phone numbers. After a few phone conversations, I invited them over for lunch and prepared one of our specialty dishes, Sabzi Chalau, spinach and rice.

On a young and luminescent summer day, I was invited to their house for coffee. I mentioned it to Sahar and asked her to come along. I visited a flower shop before meeting with Sahar at the central bus station.

When we arrived, we rang the doorbell.

---

26   Afghan dish made with short-grain rice

Woof, woof! We heard the sound of barking. My heart leapt to my mouth.

"Don't buzz, we have to escape," I said to Sahar. I dropped the flowers by the door without thinking and we turned around and ran. Only a few steps away from the door, a large dog came after us, followed by the ladies, chasing after their dog.

JEB LOST HIS JOB and, one by one, his family moved to Toronto. There was no reason for us to stay. We heard about Vancouver, British Columbia and desired to live in a warmer climate. He applied for employment in Calgary and Vancouver. He received an offer from a restaurant in British Columbia.

In the first quarter of 1996, when the weather was cool and fresh, we journeyed to a different province of Canada. While Edmonton was asleep, we began our trip on the shoulder of the Rocky Mountains. The sun took its throne in the sky, spread its arms, warming our souls and lighting the way.

There was no feverish cry at leaving except for the phobia of goodbye itself. I simply picked up all my good memories and looked forward to the change. Jeb drove while Dad sat in the passenger seat. Mom and I were in the back seat with Yuseuf. He was too young to understand the reason for relocation. I held most of his toys and colouring books on my lap to keep him entertained.

Daylight introduced us to the outskirts of the Rocky Mountains as we drove on its belt towards British Columbia. The greenery twined on both sides as we moved towards prosperity. British Columbia displayed its artistic scenery. Nature spoke in a wave of energy and our jaws dropped in awe.

I put my hand on my tummy, challenging nature's beauty.

"I'm pregnant."

* *

MY PARENTS MOVED TO a one-bedroom apartment in the building beside ours. Yuseuf started preschool and took his first step on the path of education. I took a position at a clothing store near our apartment. The little being inside me was growing, preparing his way out to the world, and my stomach started protruding.

On the third week of autumn, labor pain disturbed our morning routine. We dropped everything and rushed to the hospital. It all came as a new experience. Jeb got Mom while Dad stayed home with Yuseuf.

Jeb and Mom were in the room with me at the hospital. I refused the epidural during the thirteen hours of labor.

"Mrs. Mehdawi, one more push," I heard the doctor demanding.

A tiny voice cried, "Hello, world."

The doctor announced, "It's a boy."

I literally felt as if the universe itself stood before me to recite its most beautiful sonnet. I listened to creation's poetry. Words cannot express the emotion of that moment, nor can any artist paint, photograph, or produce a poem to capture that scene. You have to be a mother to feel it.

The nurses cleaned and wrapped him in a blue baby blanket and put him in my arms. I held my own flesh and blood. All of my pain and agony once again faded. His round brown eyes, his full, black head of hair, and his innocence made me fall in love at once. I kissed his tiny hands.

"Thank you for coming to this world to be by my side and make our family complete." I pressed him to my chest. We named him Elias to be used in both English and Farsi-Dari.

⁂

IN MID SPRING, I received a letter from Frau Bors. It was an invitation to celebrate her birthday.

I was reluctant, but Mom and Jeb said, "We'll take care of the kids. You need a break. Go."

So, I flew to Germany to join her on her memorable day. The celebration started with church mass followed by a luncheon at a fancy restaurant. I met with the principal and some of the teachers from Realschule where I was a guest student. The past paraded before my eyes. I stayed in Germany for one week with Arash, Siawash, and Aunt Razia. I also visited Dr. Olk and some other places I'd worked.

On my return from Germany a few friends visited us. It's a cultural tradition that friends and family pay a visit on a return from a trip.

"We admire you how left your children and went alone, good for you," my friend said, "We could not do such thing."

Her comment guilt-tripped me and left me sleepless for a couple nights. *Did I neglect my children? A mother should never do things like that. Am I a bad mother?*

The births of both my children watered the seed of cultural attitudes inside memory and more. Not only did I want to be a perfect mother and raise perfect children, I valued others opinions of me.

I signed up myself and Yuseuf at the library near our apartment. One afternoon, we visited the library and I noticed a room with several computers.

I approached the front desk and asked, "Excuse me, are those computers for everyone to use?"

"If you're a member, you can use it for one hour," the librarian said, "And if it's not busy, you can sign up with a different computer for another hour."

"Thank you, can you please show me?" I asked.

I was familiar with computers from my accounting studies so I started searching for accounting jobs.

◆◆

A FEW YEARS LATER, Mom and Dad flew to Germany to visit Arash and Siawash. They saw Arash after thirteen years of separation and seven years for Siawash. I asked Mom and Dad to meet Frau Bors. Siawash arranged for their gathering and invited Frau Bors over for dinner. I requested that Mom cook one of my and Frau Bors's favorite dishes, Qabili Palau, rice with raisins, and carrots, that I'd introduced her to. Frau Bors invited them back on a Sunday afternoon.

I asked Frau Bors numerous times to visit me in Canada, but she always refused and said, "Parastu, you have lots of responsibilities. You come to Germany anytime you want."

I found a full-time job as a data entry clerk. I had a perfect shift from seven in the morning until three in the afternoon. I had half a day to pursue my duties as a mother, wife, and daughter.

Jeb and I both worked full time, and we both learned from coworkers that we could invest in a house. We met with the bank and qualified for the loan. After many years of employment and schooling we bought a house in Surrey, British Columbia and moved in with our parents.

Our district was family and multi-culturally oriented, with lots of kids on our street. Most of the children were of the same age and went to the same elementary school. The neighbourhood children played outside after school. It was a safe community. Many parents also established good relationships. They socialized and supported one another in times of need.

The sunny weather of a Sunday afternoon invited kids outside, and they planned a hockey match. Hockey was very popular in the neighbourhood. Whether they were part of a league or not, most kids owned a hockey stick, and some even had a net. Elias and Yuseuf had full gear for a player and goalie.

The street we lived on had a cul-de-sac in the middle, and the area was sheltered for the kids to play hockey. Elias was a goalie, and Yuseuf and the other kids were players.

The golden day also lured me outside, so I decided to walk around the block. I left the house and the noise of children, which filled the air. I breathed into my essence.

As I made my way around the block, I stopped to watch the kids play hockey. I heard a voice coming towards me.

"Hi, Para!" Para was a nickname for me. It was a neighbor boy, whose brother was a friend of my children. He was playing with an action figure on the curb side. I smiled at him and greeted him back.

"My brother entered my room without my permission, and I am not going to talk to him," he said.

My heart melted with this openness, and I moved my attention from the hockey scene and offered him my full attention.

"Did you ask him why?"

"No," he said.

"The best thing is to talk to him and ask him why."

He agreed to what I'd suggested and resumed playing with his toys. I was still on the curb when I saw his mom walking towards us with a bag of groceries.

"Hello, Para," she said.

"Hello, how are you? Isn't it a beautiful day?"

"I'm good. And yes, it is gorgeous," she answered and moved closer. Before she reached me though, her son rushed forward and stopped her, explaining our earlier conversation.

"Mom, Para gave me excellent advice on my brother. Para suggested that I should talk to my brother and ask him the reason."

His mom looked straight at her son's eyes and said, "Son, this is our problem to deal with. Only your Dad and I can give you advice."

Blood rushed to my face, and my eyes froze in their sockets. I begged my ego carry me home.

"How is work, Para? How are your parents?" she proceeded to ask.

"They're good, work is good too," I answered, and my voice wavered. "Nice to see you, I have to go, bye."

I walked home and thought back to my teenage years.

"BEBE, AGHA[27]!" GULALI ENTERED the foyer and yelled.

"Yes, Gulali?" Mom answered.

"Modeer[28] Sahib[29] and his family are at the door and they want to see you," she said. Modeer Sahib was the principal and one of our neighbors.

The living room door opened, and they were greeted by Mom and Dad. Mom quickly came out of the room.

"Get Gulali, and both of you prepare tea with cookies." It was around two in the afternoon of Friday. I changed and grabbed Gulali.

I entered the living room, said good afternoon, and went to Modeer Sahib and his wife, who were in their sixties, and kissed their hands. Their son, a gentleman in his early thirties, stood up and I greeted him with a handshake.

I made two trips to the kitchen to bring cookies and tea. With each entry to the living room, I heard them discussing their son who wanted to get married again. I was not supposed to sit with them since it was a grown-up issue. So I left the room, but my curiosity encouraged me to hide behind the dining room curtains to eavesdrop.

"Ahang Sahib, our son in the name of God has three girls. He wants to have a son who can inherit the family name," Modeer Saheeb said. "We have chosen a girl who we know is from a respectable family, and he's also agreed to marry her. We're going to their house to ask for her hand, and we want you to come with us."

---

27   Slang, a nickname that means *sir*

28   Principal

29   People's careers used as a title of esteem

"Of course, I will come," Father said.

"Ostad[30]," the older woman referred to Mom's title as a professor, "Can you please join us too?"

"Are we going now?" Mom asked.

"Yes, if it is okay with you," the older man said.

Mom and Dad excused themselves to get changed. I quickly ran to the kitchen and pretended to help Gulali with the dishes.

"HOORAY! WE WON, WE won, we won!" the cheerful sound of kids captured my thoughts and I passed through the idyllic world of the neighbourhood children and went home.

---

30   Teacher

Chapter Twelve

Culture and society added further weight to my core as my children began their adolescence. I visited the library more often. *Chicken Soup for Teenage Soul, How to Parent a Teen,* these books helped me understand the realm of today's teenagers. I ordered the audiotape of Dr. F. Holakouee, an Iranian psychologist and sociologist, about anxiety and teens. I paid extra attention to coworkers and friends with teens.

"Kids should be involved in sports to keep them safe from bad influences," a coworker advised.

I hired a tutor to help my children with their studies. She was an experienced schoolteacher who also tutored.

One day after tutoring, I asked, "Any tips on teenagers?"

She smiled and said, "From age thirteen until seventeen, teenagers display such completely different behaviour, that you will not be able to recognize them." She laughed and continued, "Once they turn seventeen, they will get back to normalcy, and you will have your sons back."

Yuseuf was thirteen years old, and Elias was three years younger. It was the summer holidays. At around 8 a.m., I got up to make breakfast for Yuseuf before his friend arrived to drive him to basketball camp. Yuseuf and his friend had signed up for summer camp. For one week, they had basketball camp every day. His friend's dad agreed to driving them back and forth, which was at least a thirty-minute drive from our place.

Swimming was another summer activity. I signed up both Yuseuf and Elias for lessons. After work, I drove them to the swimming pool. One afternoon, they arranged to stay at the pool with friends for swimming. I welcomed the idea. I packed snacks and my swimsuit too. I drove Yuseuf and Elias, along with two of their friends, to the pool. I changed into my swimsuit to guard them from a distance.

I travelled in between pools, "I'm so sorry," I repeated as I bumped into swimmers while my eyes followed the direction of my kids. I had this feeling they should be visible at all times.

The season of freedom was upon us. The sharp edge of morning shined on the neighbourhood. The doorbell rang. Yuseuf opened the door and ran upstairs.

"Mom, Mom, where are you?"

"Hey, Baba[31] Jaan, I am in the kitchen," I replied.

"Mom, can Elias and I go play soccer with some friends?" Yuseuf asked.

"Who's playing?" I asked.

"Some of the kids from our street and my friend from school and his brother," Yusuef answered.

"How old is his brother?" I asked quietly.

"Come on, Mom, my friends are waiting. He is older than us," Yuseuf answered impatiently.

---

31   Nickname for males

"Of course, Baba Jaan, and watch out for your brother," I added.

The school was a ten-minute walk from our home. I heard them screaming with joy. The excitement of their adventure brought joy to my bones. I moved to the living room window and watched them carry the hockey net and a soccer ball, teasing one another and bursting into laughter.

After a good twenty minutes, I grabbed my car keys and drove to the school field, parking somewhere the kids could not see me. I policed them for a bit to ensure their safety.

Hockey in winter, swimming in summer, basketball and roller hockey in spring, were all part of my kids' yearly activities and my vanity. During playoffs, if it happened to be out of town, we turned it into a mini-vacation, and all four of us drove together and stayed overnight. I sought extra solace whenever I dropped my kids off at their friends' houses. I spent time at the theatre or recreation center and picked them up after. We also welcomed their friends for sleepovers. As I walked the path of my childrens' adolescence, I reminisced about my own teenage years.

❧

ON A FRIDAY AFTERNOON, someone knocked on our door. It was Uncle Mir, Sahar's dad, accompanied by Sahar and Bebe Kalan, my grandmother. Mom and Dad greeted them. I hugged Sahar and we went to my room. It was winter break, Sahar and I had both finished grade five.

Uncle did not stay, he just dropped them off and said, "I will be back next Friday to pick you guys up."

Mom and Dad said goodbye and helped Grandma upstairs. The following Friday came and went, and Uncle did not show up. The second week passed by. Still no sign of Uncle.

Sahar and I were thrilled that our sleepover had been stretched out by my Uncle's absence. Sahar and I secretly hoped she could stay longer, and we could have more fun.

I saw the disquieting gaze of my parents with the additional length of their stay, but I could not associate it with anything wrong. I could not see the red and puffy eyes of my mom. I simply ignored it to enjoy my holiday.

After twenty straight sleepovers, Mom said, "Sahar, your mom called last night, and she wants you to get back home."

I turned to Sahar and said, "No way."

Sahar said nothing but got up with teary eyes to pack her bag. Sahar and I whined at parting but were happy that we were all going to their house. Dad went out to get a taxi, and we all got in for a trip to Uncle's house in Karte Char, a different town of Kabul.

The cab stopped by the front door and my father paid the driver. Sahar ran faster than all of us to get home but the door was locked. It was a small metal door attached to a garage gate. She knocked and their housekeeper opened the door.

To my surprise, Uncle's car, an old, blue Cutlass was parked inside the garage. Two buildings sat opposite of one another, kept apart by a beautiful garden. We crossed the garden and went to Grandma's house. I saw that Aunt Razia and my other uncle, my mom's brother, and all their children were there. Sahar's mom was sitting on the mattress across from the foyer with her two sons at her two sides. Nobody moved to welcome us. None of our cousins ran outside to greet us.

What is this surprise? I wondered.

It was a kingdom of silence.

Grandma's room included both a family room and her bedroom. It was a decent size, her single bed in the left corner. The mattress had matching pillows, all in red with black flowers.

Grandma's eyes were caged with tears. She scanned the room at once.

"What is going on? Why are you all here?" Grandma rushed to Sahar's mom, who tried to get up out of respect to greet her. Bebe Kalan grabbed her hand and demanded an answer. "Where is Mir? Why all of you are silent?"

My mom held Grandma from behind, concerned about her health. "Mom, please sit down, first."

Grandma mourned in misery, "Where is Mir? What are you guys hiding from me?" she continued, "Perwin, I swear to you by my white head, I require the truth."

Mom kneeled down in front of her, "Mom, Mom. Mir has been imprisoned by the government."

The calm before the storm shattered and the tragic scene unfolded before us. Sahar ran to her mom, hugged her by the neck, and burst into tears. My grandmother was pulling her hair in sorrow and screaming her son's name out loud with tears.

"Mir, how can I live without you? Who will take care of your wife and three children?" She screamed, "You were supposed to bury me, Mir, Mir."

Every adult in the room, including Sahar and her two brothers, was sobbing. I took refuge on the mattress beside the entrance door, where all the other kids crowded.

My parents were the first people notified of this appalling act. Dad tried his best to find out where the government had taken Uncle Mir. But Uncle was nowhere to be found. Dad realized what had happened and asked my mom and uncle's wife to let Grandma know. We stayed at Sahar's house until late in the afternoon, and all we did was stare at one another from across the room.

"Bobo gul," Dad said, "Please beg your son, Sahar's dad, and make him swear by your white hair that he will watch his mouth and not to say anything against the government." Dad pleaded with Grandma a few months after the communist government took power. "The Democratic Khalq and Parcham party is campaigning for an anti-government abolition and they have their spies everywhere. They're recording people's conversations and any wrong thing said will lead to imprisonment without trial." He also begged his own mom to swear her son would watch what he said.

Father's nine family members, including his own brother, were incarcerated and slaughtered without committing any crime.

"Perwin Jaan, this Khalq and Parcham government have no mercy on people. They are tyrants. They butcher and kill right away anyone who is imprisoned. I have no power left in me to go through imprisonment ever again. I want you to get some poison from the pharmacy. If they put me in jail, I'll finish myself off before the government." Dad told Mom once as I snooped.

One Friday afternoon, as I served Dad and his friends tea and cookies, I overheard them talking.

"The government dug an immense abyss and pushes prisoners down the holes to bury them alive. It's called a mass graveyard."

My knees trembled and I noticed that they had paused. I quickly placed the tea pot with cookies on the table and left. I wanted to know more. I entered the dining room and hid behind the curtains.

A soldier who was at the scene explained how the ground moves from the live bodies and you hear their cries, screams, and moaning from underground.

"This is an act of inhumanity."

Sweat rushed to my forehead and goosebumps formed on my arms.

"Mom, I am scared. can I sleep in your room?" I asked. I could not even close my eyes without picturing that scene on that night.

I used to get up before everyone else to get ready for school. When I went to the family room to set up the table for breakfast, I could see the ashtray full of Dad's cigarette butts.

At night, Father listened to the BBC Farsi-Dari channel, broadcasted outside the country, to get the true details of war and surroundings. It was a small radio operated by battery, Father put it near his ear or held it in his hand to listen.

"Do not mention at school that we have access to the BBC News," Father emphasized to us.

The war between the government and Mujahedeen was a day's theme. At school we were told to listen to the news in the evening and share it in class.

"The government defeated the last attempt of Mujahedeen and coupons for flour and oil were handed out to soldiers' families." I presented these two pieces of information over and over.

Bang! Arash and I dropped to the floor.

"Don't move! Stay on the ground!" Mom and Dad screamed, running to the family room on their knees. Darkness cloaked the family room in the late afternoon of a summer day. I was on the mattress beside Arash. I could only see not hear anything. A bullet was fired. It crashed through the window, passed over our heads, and hit the wall. The gunman could have aimed one inch lower and claimed our lives.

We lived on a battlefield without law. A human's life was as worthless as a fly's on the wall. We did not know what happened or who did it. Was it targeted or random? It remained a mystery.

I was fourteen years old, going on fifteen. Our school days were six days of the week, for four hours each day.

On Saturday morning, the teacher announced, "This Thursday, school will be closed for maintenance." The entire class fell in a deep soundless emotion. The bell rang and we all let out hoorays.

"The community swimming pool is open seven days a week for men and once a week for women only," my friend Kahkashan said. She continued, "On Thursday, we could go swimming. Can you come and you can sleep over at my place?"

"I have to ask Mom and Dad," I said.

Kahkashan lived in Macrorayan, and I lived in Karte Parwan, two different cities. Macrorayan town was more modern, with apartments with warm water for showering, at least once a week.

"You can go, but return before it gets dark," Mom said.

"Mom, Khakashan said that I could sleep over at her house, can I?"

"I trust you and we know she is a very good girl from a respected family, but people talk and judge." She stretched on a proverb, "Do not leverage people's knife."

I got the answer.

From Karte Parwan to Macrorayan was about an hour and a half bus ride and sometimes, with traffic jams, it could take two hours. I had to change buses at the city center. I wrapped my arms around myself. Going out in public felt like playing Russian roulette. Women could get groped and harassed verbally. Targeted bomb explosions on the city bus and crowded areas was another anxiety to face.

I asked myself, am I brave enough to travel? The vibrant images of long summer days with its therapeutic heat, walking around the pool with Kahkashan, reading poetry and books alleviated my fear of the city center.

I carried some extra clothes and packed a mystery novel to return to Kahkashan along with the two new prose poems I wrote titled, *Moon* and *Longhair*, and left the house. Morning turned to noon, and I arrived in Macrorayan.

I quickly changed at Kahkashan's home, and off we went to the pool. The place was packed with women of all ages. Primarily women from the upper class—or at least, they were acting like that. Some had swimsuits on, with their hair fixed in curls, either short or long, wearing full makeup and taking puffs of their cigarettes. The pool was twenty meters in length and forty feet wide, and it also had areas to sit under the shade. Concession stands sold snacks and ice cream. It was my very first time visiting that center.

We purchased our tickets, entered the club, and got a place in the shadow of a tree. Kahkashan laid the picnic blanket on the ground and filled it with the food she'd packed from home. I did not have a swimsuit, nor did Kahkashan. I was wearing jeans with a button-up red shirt. I rolled my jeans up. Kahkashan and I, just for the sake of fashion, wrapped small Indian shawls with gold glitter around our waists. I freed my hair from my hair ties and put on some lipstick. We finished eating and started walking around the pool. We waved at familiar faces and stopped by friends who also went to Zarghona High School.

"Let's sit by the edge of the pool and dip our feet in the water," Kahkashan said.

We leaned back on our hands and plunged our legs in the water. The cold of the pool caressed my bones, and my legs danced with the waves. The deep anxiety of the sun moving west ended my composure.

"I have to go," I said to Kahkashan. "It will get dark if I don't leave now."

"Ah, too soon! Please stay a little longer. It is so nice here," she said.

"I know, but I have two buses to catch," I declared.

Kahkashan walked me to the gate, and she went back to the pool.

It was quarter to six when the bus stopped on the opposite side of the Baharistan Cinema in Karte Parwan. I got off while the daylight was fading in color.

The atmosphere was smoggy, and the street was pressed with people and cars. I ran to cross the road to get home faster. As I crossed, the congestion grew worse. My heart pounded while my feet hit the pavement vigorously. I pleaded with my mind to escape the crowd. The more I pushed, the more threatening the haze became. The voices of men, women and children combined with cries. My eyes shuttered.

A streak of blood on the street gave testimony of a bad incident. I forced my way up while people came down to get to the crowded area. It delayed my attempt. In all the commotion, I saw my father passing through the slope.

"Padar Jaan!" I called out.

He reached out and grabbed my hand with both palms and stared at me without a word. He gasped for air.

"A missile was shot near the tailor shop this afternoon."

⁌ ⁌

YALDA[32] WAS THE LONGEST night of the year and gave birth to winter at midnight. It was an ancient tradition that our ancestors cherished and celebrated. After dinner, Mom seeded pomegranates and put them in a basin. She mixed dried berries, walnuts, and raisins in a separate bowl and asked me to place them on top of the Sandali. A Sandali is a low table with a large quilt to cover all sides. A brazier with burnt charcoal was placed underneath the table. Dad told the history of Yalda as we sat on each side of

---

32 A Persian holiday that celebrates the longest night of the year

the Sandali and pushed our feet to touch the manqal[33], munching on dried and fresh fruits.

"Daughter, recite a Hafiz poem for us," Dad asked me.

"At the break of dawn from sorrows I was saved, In the dark night of the soul, drank the elixir I craved," I read out loud.

The school holidays along with the customary sleepover began. I packed my pajamas with a few other clothes and bused to Sahar's house. We'd both finished grade eleven.

The next day before breakfast Sahar said, "Let's ask Mom to take us to the theatre." I agreed.

"Mom, Parastu and I worked really hard at school. To honor our good grades can you take us to the theater?" Sahar outlined the plan at the breakfast table.

"Auntie, we really want to celebrate the beginning of our holiday," I said to back up our plan. With successful perseverance, she agreed to take us to the theatre.

"I hope an Indian movie plays at the Aryana Cinema," Sahar said.

We did not know which movies would play, nor did we have the showtime schedule. Sahar and I dressed up in skirts that fell below the knees, with nylons and matching sweaters. We wore high-heeled boots, shouldering the joy of adulthood. We both shared some ideas for applying face cream under our eyes and pushing them up for shaping.

"I have a brown color lipstick," I showed Sahar. We were not allowed to pluck our thick, dark eyebrows. Eyebrow shaping was

---

33 Manual heater

viewed as a sign of engagement, the same as wearing too much makeup. Auntie was pacing in the foyer.

"Sahar, Parastu, come on! Aren't you guys done?"

We both appeared in front of her. She seemed on edge. Her eyes flitted over us, and then she nodded her head in approval.

"Remember, no talk of any kinds inside the taxi," she continued to make us understand the delicacy of the circumstances, "Discussion about subjects like politics, government, or religion with strangers are open to various interpretations. One wrong word can be an invitation to danger, since we don't know if the driver is a government or Mujahideen ally. Got it?"

I swallowed and pulled on my skirt. "Of course, Auntie."

The crisp wind along with the gentle touch of the sun brushed away the fearsome images in my mind.

Auntie raised her hand up for a taxi passing by. The taxi driver asked for the address, and Auntie agreed on the cost. No words were exchanged during the ride, as planned.

The cinema was a two-story building. We purchased our tickets, and luckily showtime was within the next hour. There were no snack shops inside the theatre, but people could buy a snack outside and bring it inside.

A crowd of people were standing on the second floor by the showroom door to get inside and find their seats. We slowly climbed the stairs and noticed that everyone who passed us was male. Oh well, women might have lined up in a separate area, we thought. We stepped onto the second floor and were surprised to see there were no other women.

Auntie pulled on our arms in agitation and whispered in distress, "I got fooled by two immatures, sang ba sarim[34] hamrayee in karim!" Which means, stone on my head with this effort! Off we went down the stairs.

She went directly to the ticket seller. "My daughter got sick, we cannot watch the movie, please reimburse our ticket, brother Jaan?"

"Auntie, I can't do that," the young attendant said.

"Son, I am telling you the truth. I made an error bringing two young girls to the cinema. You are like my own son. Think of your own sisters," Auntie replied.

He started counting the money while talking, "Mother Jaan, you made a terrible mistake. No woman should leave the house in this present situation."

We thanked him and left the building with our heads hung low.

⁂

THE COMPANY I WORKED for downsized, and I got laid off. The hassle of finding another job, a mortgage payment, and all other expenses only with one income, numbed my thoughts. I bought the newspaper and looked for admin jobs in the classified sections. I had a couple of interviews lined up but never heard anything back.

"I want to go back to school," I said to Jeb after three months of unemployment. "You see, I tried to grab any position, but no luck," I added.

---

34   A slang term used in crises, meaning *stone to my head*

Jeb asked, "What are you going to study? What if you spend all that time and money and still couldn't find a job?"

"I think I want to study what I started in Germany. Last week when I took Dad to the dentist, I spoke with the assistant. She said there are lots of job openings for this career with good pay."

In 2006, I finished the one-year program and got my license as a certified dental assistant. Luckily, I was hired as an assistant after my practicum.

One day, I dropped off the kids at school on my day off and drove to the nearest shopping center. While I made a left turn at the intersection, a loud bang made my car spin 360 degrees. My head hit the airbag, and a cloud of smoke encircled me. While the car was still on, I opened the driver's door and jumped out. Then, I saw the police car in the area and a crowd of people at the scene. The ambulance entered the area and the people who'd swarmed around me dispersed.

"Ma'am, the driver of the other car admitted to his fault, but we just want to hear your side of the story as well," the police officer said.

I was hit by a pickup truck and my car was towed.

"Can I use your phone?" I asked a man nearby.

I called Jeb. I got an x-ray and was checked by the emergency doctor at the hospital later on. They released me with whiplash injuries to my neck and shoulder.

The neck and shoulder pain prevented me from practicing as an assistant, and the terror of getting back in the driver's seat troubled me.

"Jeb, can you please take me to the doctor?"

"Jeb, I have physiotherapy."

"Jeb, we need groceries."

"Jeb, Yuseuf has practice, Elias has game."

"Jeb, Jeb, Jeb."

I am a burden. After years of running a marathon without crossing the finish line, I hit rock bottom.

In the morning after the kids and Jeb left, I curled up on the couch, watching TV. The chronic feeling of emptiness triggered my tears.

◆ ◆

IT WAS EID celebration, and family and friends paid their respect by visiting my parents.

"How are you doing Parastu Jaan? Do you work? How are your kids doing?" they asked.

"Good. No. Good," I answered. I was afraid that if I elaborated, I might burst into tears.

The last book I'd read was to educate me on the realm of teenagers. I'd put the pen down after journaling and turned the page. The poetic girl inside me, with a suppressed feeling of saudade (in Portuguese folk culture), once again cried for help.

◆ ◆

THAT SAME YEAR WE sold the house and bought a new property in a different city called Maple Ridge. I tried to measure the town's safety before relocating. I called the police office as well as the school board. I was satisfied, and we moved.

I signed up with some temping agencies to get some occasional shifts as a dental assistant. I accepted any shifts on any day and got a ride with Jeb.

Jeb found some Persian stores selling books on the Vancouver North Side and introduced it to my father. Father steadily began purchasing books and formed his own wall-to-wall library, since he'd left behind his own library back home, which contained almost a thousand volumes of books on different subjects.

The Afghan Society introduced themselves to my father. The association supported cultural and traditional events and served the Afghan population in the province. They taught a few classes at a secondary school on Saturdays to teach Farsi-Dari to young children. It was all volunteer work by people who used to teach back home.

On a hot summer day, the Afghan community representative visited my father. I served them tea with cookies.

"Ahang Sahib," the representative said, "We want to establish a history class and we need your support. Can you teach history to the young Afghans?"

"With honor," he pointed at his library and continued, "This library belongs to all Farsi-Dari speaking people who desire to read."

Mom and Dad also built a circle of friends who visited them on a regular basis and borrowed books.

"Any time I borrow a book from Ahang Sahib, I make sure first, to finish it fast, and second, to understand it well, since I know he will ask questions," a friend once said.

Father, Yuseuf, and Elias headed to the Saturday classes. I registered my kids to get basic knowledge of the grammar and written language of Farsi-Dari.

We'd passed two seasons since we'd moved to this new town, and spring was at our doorstep. I heard the Earth's pulse and smelled the fresh scent of the air and opened the window. The chirping birds hinted that it was time to cultivate my own garden.

One night my dad told us, "On March 8th, the Afghan community is celebrating Women's Day. I told the community representative that you would recite a poem that day."

"Wow, that's nice,' I said.

"I pulled some poetry books that you can choose from," Dad replied.

"Asif[35] Jaan, they just came from work. She can look later," said Mom.

"Of course. I am not saying now," he said, returning to his book.

I looked through the books Dad picked out. One book that captured my attention was *Afghan Women Poets*. I turned the pages and a poem by Nadia Anjuman[36] stood tall before my eyes.

"Padar Jaan, what do you think of these lyrics?" I read it out loud.

"That is a very strong verse, nice pick," Dad said.

"This poem shows the torture and pain Afghan women have endured over the centuries. It's so appalling. Inhumane. And the sad part is that it keep happening." My voice thickened. "Media, history, and the world have been writing and broadcasting about

35   Dad's name

36   Afghan poet

their pain and suffering, but nothing gets done. It's just a myth to the world. Why Dad? When does it end? Why?" I cried.

My father took the book from me to write the poem down and heaved a big sigh.

I practiced reciting the poem in front of the mirror:

> *"No desire to voice my pain; what should I scream about?*
> *I have been hated for centuries; either I scream or keep silence.*
> *I know it's spring, the season of blooming,*
> *How can I fly when my wings are folded, tied?"*

• •

THREE THINGS DEFINED ME back home. I was skinny, shy, and a storyteller. Sahar's dad used to call me the family's speaker. In Germany, when Sahar's oldest brother hosted a Nowruz celebration, he performed music and invited me to recite a poem.

The afternoon of March 8th, I put on a black capri pant suit with a white shirt, put on make-up, and painted my lips with a soft orange color lipstick, and we left the house.

I took my children to participate in these celebrations to gain experience and be around the Afghan community. I introduced them to the Persian poets Hafiz, Ferdousi, Jami, Nezami and Saadi, the five pillars of Farsi-Dari poetry. I feasted at Nowruz and honored other cultural events, especially for my children to commemorate their roots and observe both cultures.

We were greeted by friends and other important members of the Afghan community, considering my father was with us. We walked to a table that stood at the heart of the hall.

The ceremony began with the leader of the association's speech. The night was separated into two segments. The first part included poetry and addresses, the second was a coffee break followed by music.

A few people went on the stage to read their speeches and poems they picked from other poets or wrote themselves.

The host called my name, "We are going to invite Parastu Ahang-Mehdawi to proceed to the stage and recite the poem she chose for us."

I did not look at anyone, just grabbed the folder and got up at once. I could hear my heartbeat race. I climbed one, two, three stairs before arriving in the spotlight. The podium with its sharp gaze coerced me to take my spot.

Click, click, click. The sound of my high heels echoed on the stage. I arrived behind the podium and pulled out the paper with Dad's handwriting, tilting the microphone towards my mouth, a lesson from the toastmaster class that I'd taken as a student. I raised my head and looked at the audience to gain control. The crowd was busy with their company. Some moved around, socializing with friends, while others enjoyed the group gathered around the table.

Arrows of sound shot from every corner, and I thought, how can I reduce the volume of this loud environment? How high should I raise my voice? My gaze locked on Yuseuf and Elias, who sat patiently, waiting for their mom to start. An eminent feeling poked me to the core, and I began, "In the name of God of wisdom, greetings to each and every one of you, I am honoured." My legs trembled, but it did not crack my voice. I noticed that the guests paid attention to the wave of sound and some moved back to their seats. The room slowly fell into a deep silence. Confidence raised my shoulders high, and my voice reached the ceiling. I finished the delivery and thanked the audience.

When I reached my seat, Yuseuf and Elias both walked to me. "Mom, you did good," Yuseuf said.

Elias followed his brother and also said, "Mom, you did good."

"Thanks, Baba Jaan," I answered both my kids. My gaze wandered to my parents and Jeb, who showed their support.

A line formed in front of the kitchen. Some community members stood up to join the group, but instead, they shifted their direction and strolled towards our table.

"Parastu Jaan, salaam, that was a great performance. You made us cry. We are proud of you," they said.

I stood before them and thought I grew taller with each word that came out of their mouths.

I continued visiting my dad's library and picked up books on literature and poetry. The two books that had travelled with me from region to region rested snugly in my own library beside the parenting books.

I resumed with full-time employment as a receptionist and temped as dental assistant.

"Do you still fear driving?" a coworker asked.

"Yes, when I see cars in the opposite direction, a big bang sound crashes in my ear," I answered.

"Why don't you talk to a psychologist about this and share all your fears?" she suggested.

Jeb went back to school and got a diploma in computer programming and had some part-time shifts on Friday nights and the weekend.

On a late afternoon, I lay down on the couch and searched for Opera Winfrey's show. The show started with an announcement that viewer discretion was advised. I was extra curious to find out what the show was about. It was her interview with Nobel Peace prize winner, Elie Wiesel, a Holocaust survivor.

They showed the Auschwitz camp, and Elie explained how he pinched himself to remind himself that he was alive. Elie spoke about his book *Night* and his message to the leaders and the world as a political activist and writer.

He said, "Our lives no longer belong to us alone. They belong to all those who need us desperately."

The show ended and I gasped for air, running to the balcony. It was a lot to take in. It felt like all creation was suspended. With eyes wide open, I saw the injustice before my eyes, screaming for help. People from my homeland, slavery, the Holocaust, and on and on. Nonstop tears washed my face as an urge to write triggered my essence. I picked up the pen and wrote an essay about Determinism and Freewill in Farsi-Dari and wondered, what is our life really about, and why does war exist?

◆◆

SATURDAY MORNING, I PARKED the car and went into the dental office. The receptionist called the assistant.

"Morning Parastu, is that right? Am I pronouncing it correctly?"

"Yes you are. You can also call me Para, to make it easier."

"Parastu is not hard," she said, "Anyway, the ortho assistant called in sick. Do you have an ortho module?"

"No, I don't," I answered.

"It's okay. Just assist with the basics, can you?" she asked.

"Of course I can."

I undraped the last scheduled patient and walked him to the reception area, then walked back to the room to sterilize. The dentist was charting. I paused as I was wiping the counter and collecting the instruments.

"Can I ask you something?" I asked the dentist.

"Sure," the dentist said.

"I want to take my module, do you know where I can do that?"

The dentist turned around and faced me. "You should. I will give you the contact information."

I filled out the application and got registered for the program. It ran through the University of British Columbia. The practicum of the program was held at the Nobel Biocare Oral Health Centre, and I noticed that there were dental assistants who were employees.

I obtained the clinic's phone number and called to introduce myself.

"I am looking for dental assistant positions and would love to work at the clinic of dentistry."

"There are a few positions available that we just posted. Apply online."

I did apply.

A couple of days later, I was invited for an interview. I drove one and a half hours from Maple Ridge to the university. I arrived early and prepared myself for the interview. A couple of days later, they called back and offered me the University of British Columbia position.

The sound of this title, university, was like an open wound. It presented itself in my thoughts, but the campus atmosphere watered the dried soil of a lost dream.

On September 17, 2009, I left the house at five in the morning; my shift started at 7:30. I drove to the nearest Starbucks coffee shop and ordered coffee and a muffin. I seized a chair across from the entrance door.

I was drawn to every single person who stepped in, and I assumed a connection with them. I ached to just salute each and every one of them for achieving their goal. I beamed and took a sip of the coffee. I fed my pride with the deep flavours of Americano and the sweet taste of a blueberry muffin.

The clock challenged me with its ticking and reminded me to get to work. I pushed the coffee shop door open with vigor. The daylight pulled the dark curtain of night aside, and the sun said hello. The sky dressed in beds of cloud. The trees traveled with me in honour of my first day. The birds guided us through the unknown places, and I arrived.

Chapter Thirteen

I walked hand in hand with my children on the path of adolescence. Deep down, I was still a bewildered teenager, a young girl who'd blossomed in spring, ripened in summer, envisioned in autumn, and dwelled in winter. Who was I?

Art traveled in our house and wove into our souls. Music vibrated through the air. Pop and hip hop beats echoed. I relished the English hits and formed playlists. Beyoncé and Ed Sheeran stirred my desire to weep and dance.

Yuseuf showed an interest in rapping, and he even recorded a few rap songs. He also had good taste in fashion. He introduced me to some of the brand names that I hadn't paid any attention to before. We bonded with one another on movie nights.

"Mission Impossible," Elias called out.

"Nice. Good one," Yuseuf and Jeb said.

"Mom, do you like it?" they asked.

"Of course. What is the genre?" I asked.

"Action," Elias said.

I took my spot on the mattress beside the fireplace. Ten minutes, then thirty minutes passed by and then the sound of the movie sounded distant, then fell completely silent.

"Mom, are you sleeping?" Elias asked.

"No, no Baba Jaan," I answered as I tried to sit upright and shake off sleep.

"Mom, you don't have to watch. Go to sleep," they said.

"Thank you, Baba Jaan. Honestly, I was not watching." I removed myself and heard them laughing.

Academy Awards became a tradition in our home, primarily for Elias and me. On a typical Oscar Sunday, I came up with excuses to avoid any engagements. I made sure to finish all my chores before 4 p.m. Pacific time. Lunch and dinner were served around 3 p.m., followed by snacks on the kitchen counter. I put my pajamas on and called it a day. When the arrows of the clock took their place on the four and twelve, I fluffed up the pillow behind my head and lay down beside the fireplace.

The red carpet, the dresses, the new styles put ideas into my head.

"Elias, the show starts in a few minutes."

I immersed myself in acceptance speeches. I rose to my feet when Meryl Streep won Best Actress and said, "I really want to thank all my colleagues, all my friends. I look out here, and you know, I see my life before my eyes," I cried.

Tears, how to describe them, I asked myself. I cannot. Tears define me.

⚬ ⚬

MY CHILDREN WERE CONSUMED by their love of sports from day one. They spent hours every day honing their talents and played on multiple teams. Jeb was fond of all types of sports, and watched hockey and basketball with the kids. I enjoyed basketball more, but I really loved being around my family. So, I did watch sports with them, especially play-offs, just to witness the joy on their faces.

A visit to Chapters Bookstore provided a sense of satisfaction. I slowly filled the lower shelf of my own library with English novels. Autobiographies and biographies fascinated me more so than fiction. I was mesmerized by reading autobiographies of influential people, such as Gandhi, Nelson Mandela, Maya Angelo, and many others.

Philosophy was another area that I was drawn to. I purchased *The Story of Philosophy* by Will Durant, but it was tough to grasp. I wrote down two of Plato's quotes in my notebook and engraved them on my heart.

The first was, "People are like the dirt; they can either nourish you and help you grow as a person, or they can stunt your growth and make you wilt and die."

The second, "Every heart sings a song, incomplete, until another heart whispers back. Those who wish to sing always find a song. At the touch of a lover, everyone becomes a poet."

◆◆

THE AFGHAN COMMUNITY CELEBRATED poetry and music on special occasions and invited me to recite. Slowly, we were introduced to Iranian poetry clubs. The community also reached out to my father to help them with a TV program broadcast on the multicultural history channel. They offered him a ten-minute segment to talk about history. Father and I, along with the Afghan association, met with the program organizer.

My Dad replied, "I can help with the material, but I cannot do the program." The community representative turned to me and asked me if I could do poetry. I discussed it with Jeb and took it under serious consideration with my busy schedule. I figured once a month would be very fitting with my hectic calendar. A ten-minute segment was offered to me. My own poetry scheme. The pen, papers, and literature swirled around me, touching the face of a little girl inside me who dressed all in white and had been asleep for decades.

I titled the poetry segment Melody of the Heart, or Tarana haye del in Farsi-Dari. For the program's intro, I recited a poem from the most influential figure in Persian literature, Ferdowsi.

"In the name of the Lord of both wisdom and mind, to nothing sublime can thought be applied."

✦✦

I ARRANGED FOUR PROGRAMS and recorded them all at once to be broadcasted once a month. The programs were: Books and their influence, The Introduction of Farsi-Dari, Plateau of Iran's language, its origin, and controversy, Hafiz: my all-time favorite poet, and Silent Heroes: my grandmother who, in King Amanullah Khan's years, was the first woman to take her burka off.

✦✦

YUSEUF WAS IN HIS twelfth year of schooling, and it was the most crucial year. It felt like I was in grade twelve as well. He made every effort to get into university, but only the University of British Columbia. I educated myself, fishing for information from academic advisors and some of my friends.

Yuseuf made it very clear, "I am interested in the School of Business. I'll apply only for business."

I could not argue with his strong will. I was imprisoned by the herd mentality. On my day off, I picked up the phone and called student services at the university.

"Hello, how can I help you?"

"I would like to get information on Medicine, Engineering and Business," I articulated.

I was transferred to all different advisors, but they all said the same thing.

"Ma'am it's all about what your son chooses, what he wants to pursue and what makes him happy."

Yuseuf applied and asked if he could talk to us about something. "Mom, Dad, I want to experience the life of a young student living in the university housing." He continued, "I would like to apply for housing and move there."

I thought of *The Prophet* by Gibran Khalil Gibran, and his amazing poem about children. "Your children are not your children. They are the sons and daughters of life longing for itself; they come through you but not from you." I heard Gibran Khalil Gibran loud and clear.

Jeb and I looked at one another and said, "Go for it, Baba Jaan."

On May of 2011, around 7:30 p.m., I returned home from thirteen hours of work including the commute. Yuseuf opened the door and greeted me.

"Mom, I have sad news," he continued: "Unfortunately, the university did not accept me. They denied me."

The entire house moved around me.

University denied me, university, denied, denied, the words echoed all around me.

I dropped the backpack in the foyer and grabbed onto the stair railing. I climbed the stairs and let go of the railing. Elias was lying down on the couch across from the TV in the family room. On the large island table, in the middle of the kitchen, sat the envelope. Yuseuf raced forward and grabbed the paper and handed it to me with a gloomy face.

I pulled the letter out of the envelope: "CONGRATULATIONS, we are happy to inform you that..."

I did not read the rest. I grabbed Yuseuf by the shoulder, hugged him, and started kissing him.

"You! You played it well, I am proud of you," I said. Tears of jubilation danced over my face and wet Yuseuf's cheeks.

Elias smiled and said, "Mom, you are crying! I thought you would be happy."

Yuseuf and Elias both laughed and said, "Mom, we love you."

I ran down the stairs and shouted, "Yuseuf got accepted at the University of British Columbia!"

Jeb, who came before me, accompanied Mom and Dad in their living room and started grinning.

"You are crying! We knew you would, congratulations!"

Obviously, everyone knew it except me. My eyes were still the host of joyful tears. I sneaked out to my room and, with the lights off, sat on the floor and cried.

In September, when the dawn rose over the city of Maple Ridge and the sun stood above the mountain ranges that wrapped around the province of British Columbia, I opened my eyes to a new experience. It felt as if the world had just been created. No dreariness, no sorrows, no war, no separation anxiety; it was only existence and love.

Yuseuf headed to university. We packed the car with his items, and off we drove to the University of British Columbia. The 94.5 station played an upbeat song. I turned the volume up, put my arms in the air, and moved with the rhythm. Jeb was driving and followed the beat, trying to chant it. Yuseuf contemplated, looking out his window.

"Mom, when we say goodbye, please don't cry."

I turned towards him. "Why would I cry Baba Jaan? We are so proud of you! It's your day to celebrate."

The university symbol appeared on the side of the road, and Jeb parked the car in the designated parking lot for student drop-off. Yuseuf strolled to the courtyard of the housing building, got his room key, and we helped him settle into his room.

The air was full of innovative breath. The vigor, playfulness, and energy was an exhibition of yesterday's hard work, today's achievement and tomorrow's creation. We realized Yuseuf wanted to get acquainted with his surroundings, and the university also had so many first-day surprises planned.

I hugged him and said, "Best of luck on your future endeavors. I love and am proud of you."

"Thanks, Mom, love you too."

To his surprise, he found his Mom's eyes all dry. Jeb and Elias said their goodbyes too. As soon as we got into the car, I pushed the CD player button and freed my tears. The famous Ahmad Zahir, an Afghani singer, was a true catharsis and blasted, "Love you forever, love you forever."

The following week on Monday morning, the bus stopped at the central station of the University of British Columbia at around 7:15 a.m. I got off the bus and walked towards the Dentistry building. As I walked, I searched the student's faces for Yuseuf. I exhaled with the elation of being in the same territory as my son.

One of my coworkers, who knew about my son's acceptance to university, approached me with a smile. "How was your son's transition? How was his first weekend at the campus?"

My eyes teared up. "It was great."

"Para, you should be happy that you've done such a good job raising a son who takes education so seriously and who got into one of the highest-ranking universities in the country."

Her son was already a student and lived at the university housing. She continued, "Para, be proud that your job is done. He is an adult now. From now on, it is his journey and life decisions."

Towards the end of autumn, on a Saturday morning, I squeezed my eyes shut. I have always been a light sleeper, my brain shifting between dreams and wakefulness. I counted on my fingers the hours of broken sleep I'd gotten. I went to the washroom and opened the window. A sudden gust crossed the window and tried to enter my lungs.

As I held onto the comforter around me, my mind dwelled with the waves of the wind. It was quiet upstairs; Elias and Jeb were still dreaming. I walked to the kitchen when a sudden thought whisked through the window of my brain, and I rushed back to the bedroom. I changed and grabbed my bag which carried *Infidel by Ayan Hirsi Ali*, a notebook, and a pen. I walked downstairs. Dad was sitting on a mattress laid beside his wall-to-wall library. He lifted his head, his luminous expression was a positive start to my day.

"Salam, Padar Jaan," I said.

"Salam my daughter, where are you going?" he asked.

"I am going for coffee," I answered and closed the door behind me.

I parked the car in front of the coffee shop near our house. I grabbed my stuff and entered the shop. A few people stood in the line and I joined them.

"What would you like?" the barista asked.

"Can I have an extra-large coffee, black with milk and sugar on the side, please?"

"Anything to eat?" she asked.

"I don't know, I don't have much of an appetite in the morning. What should I eat?"

"Look at the board and choose from our menu."

"Can I have a multi-grain bagel with light cream cheese?"

"Is it for here or to go?"

"For here, thanks."

I collected my order from the other end of the bar while I looked around, thinking, where should I sit? This was the most challenging part, where to sit. I asked myself why it was not important before. I inspected the shop, it had two seating areas on either side of the entrance door.

A lust to sit beside the window with the natural light struck me, and I seized an empty seat, gazing out the window for a good few minutes.

A couple of hours passed by, drinking my coffee and thinking. My mind wandered over Elias's crucial years. The coffee shop grew louder and I pulled my gaze from the window and turned it to the bar. A group of young hockey players rushed through the door to get donuts. My eyes met the clock and I thought it was time to resume my duties as a mother, a daughter, and a wife.

I grew accustomed to visiting the coffee shop on my days off.

"Morning Para, five dollars and eighty cents," the young man in his early twenties at the cash register said.

"How are you doing? Do you work full time?" I asked.

"Yes," he said, eyes fixated on the coffee cup. I grabbed my coffee, and he continued, "I go to college at night."

My cheeks swelled with a smile, "Good for you. I'm really happy for you."

The tray with my bagel was set down in the pickup area.

"Thanks, how are you doing?" I said to the woman.

"Para, I got my braces," she answered.

"It looks great," I replied.

I held my tray and looked around. All the spots by the window were taken. I exchanged greetings with some regular customers.

"Come, sit in your spot." A gentleman in his mid-sixties stood up from the place I usually sat.

"Oh no, please sit down. I will go on the other side," I replied.

My spirit rose and I felt at home. *Home.* I took the notebook out and began to outline the next poetry program.

An array of thoughts visited me as my coffee shop meetings persisted. I did the talking with my soul as Plato suggested. My own life journey sat before me. My childhood spoke and I drifted to adolescence. A sharp pain pierced my head as I parked my thoughts on Germany.

••

"Hi Baba Jaan," I said to Elias. He closed the car door and put his seatbelt on. "Do you want to go out for lunch?"

"Yeah, let's go, but please some place near the house. I don't want to travel far," he answered.

It was Friday, my day off. I parked the car in front of the restaurant. The host showed us to our seats and the waitress took our orders.

"How was school?" I asked.

"All good, nothing new," he answered.

"I can't believe you only have a few months of school left."

"Yes, almost done."

The waiter brought our food; burgers with fries.

"Thank you," we both said.

I took a bite of the juicy burger with the extra mushrooms mounted on top of lettuce and tomato. My stomach had a bash.

"Oh it's so good! How is yours, Baba?" I asked.

"Good," he said.

"What are your interests? Science, the arts, or business?" I asked.

"I don't know."

I took a sip of water and waited a few minutes, then continued, "What about engineering? You're terrific at math? Do you remember in elementary how your teacher always put you a grade above in math?" I asked.

He paused and said, "Yes, sure. Not bad."

We finished our food, ordered some dessert and tea, and talked about movies.

"Mom, I watched some of Leonardo Dicaprio's movies. He's so good in each of his movies. No other actor is able to bring his level of energy and excitement to a film." His posture straightened. "Mom, do you know who Marlon Brando is?"

"No Baba Jaan."

Elias's voice flooded with euphoria and he elaborated, "Marlon Brando is a famous actor. He's known for method acting. He has a documentary that I've watched several times. If you want, we can watch it together."

"Of course, Baba Jaan, we can watch it together," I replied. The waiter came to find out if we were ready for the bill.

"Mom, Marlon Brando, in his documentary, said something that echoes all around me. He said that in life you have to be somebody, if you are nobody it's a sin." His gaze turned towards the window and he said nothing else.

Elias was accepted at the University of Victoria for engineering. He took the offer and applied for university housing. The university is located in Victoria, the capital of British Columbia. Victoria was also one of my favorite places for a mini vacation. Taking the BC ferry with its spectacular scenery is so awe

-inspiring. The drive from our house to the university is about three to four hours.

It was the grade twelve graduation ceremony, and Yuseuf came home to celebrate his brother's success with us. All of us, including my parents, attended the ceremony, followed by dinner.

A table for six was reserved at the restaurant for dinner. We gathered around, speaking in both English and Farsi-Dari. Yuseuf and Elias indulged us with anecdotes of the past.

"I remember how my friends laughed when the school receptionist announced the lunchtime briefing and ended by saying, 'Elias Mehdawi to the office. Your mom brought you lunch.'" Elias said.

Yuseuf added, "I remember when Baba Asif[37] came to school to pick us up, he would not wait for us to get to him. As soon as he saw us, he would yell, 'Yuseuf, Yuseuf!' and my friends laughed."

I just sat back and let my eyes and ears remember this dreamy evening.

The following day Yuseuf had to go back to his housing at the University of British Colombia. Luckily, we both had the same destination. I decided to drive, since he had to take a few things from home with him.

We left home around 5:30 a.m. and stopped at the Tim Horton drive-through to get ourselves coffee and something to eat. We had an hour and a half to talk about his school and my work.

"I am taking philosophy, and I find it intriguing. I also admire history."

---

37 Grandpa

"Wow, that's amazing. Tell me what you have learned." My eyes bloomed.

"Mom, can I ask you a question?" he asked. "Now that Elias is done with school and takes his journey in his own hands, what are you going to do with the extra time you have?"

My neck contracted as I looked at him and then back at the road.

The music played without any interruption, and we both were quiet.

"I have never thought of this," I answered. After a good minute I continued, "I don't know. I might try to find a different job or go back to school."

Yuseuf said in a soft voice, "Mom, going back to school, or a new job, is not going to help you. You already have a job." He faced the window and continued, "Why don't you do something that your heart desires? Something you have longed for, but you never had the time nor the chance. For instance, you recite poetry. Make your own CD, record the poems you love. You love writing. Why don't you write a book? Something that makes you happy."

I dropped him off. He collected his items from the back of the car.

I hurried to hug him, and as I did he whispered, "Mom, think about what I said. You taught us to chase our dreams, why don't you?" And we parted.

In September of 2014, we sailed to Victoria to drop off Elias. I disguised my anxiety with the view and pride. Elias was thrilled, assertive, and composed—more about the housing than engineering. The university was full of young souls and their families.

Departure and goodbyes arrived before me. My children knew me very well. Elias said, "Mom, let's go back to my room and say our goodbyes."

"Of course, Baba Jaan," I replied.

Jeb and I followed him to his room. He searched my eyes for a trace of tears and failed. I hugged him.

"My Baba, I am so proud of you. You are the captain of your own destiny now." I placed the palm of my hand over my forehead and repeated, "Oh captain, my captain."

We both laughed. I showered him with kisses. Jeb hugged him and praised him, and off we went.

As we drove to catch the ferry, Jeb and I did not exchange one word. We both knew one word and I would burst in tears. I turned to face him, and we both cried at once.

The ferry appeared at the shore, we drove inside and parked, took the stairs, and off we went to the open-air deck. The view was beyond any description. The sun was sinking freely behind the hills, and as it was retiring, it enveloped my soul. I felt like a line of poetry in a sonnet read by nature.

The famous poem of Mohammad Hejazi that I'd memorized in my teens rushed through my head, and I looked around to see if anyone was close by. Tears still dwelled in my eyes and my voice thickened as I recited, "I went to the height of the mountain to kiss the eyes and ears of the moon further to place it on its throne. My eyes interpret the world into poetry and sing it in my memory."

On a Friday morning a couple of weeks after we dropped off Elias at school, I was at the coffee shop, deep in my own thoughts. A tap on my shoulder brought me back to the present.

"Ma'am, are you okay?" A man in his late fifties had approached me from behind and noticed my paralyzed stare out the window of the shop, a collection of soaked tissues in my hand, and was worried.

I smiled, "I really appreciate your concern. I am fine, just lots to think about."

He smiled back and, as he walked back to his seat, said, "Glad you're okay."

With a deep sigh, I remembered what Yuseuf advised. "Mom, follow your heart. Do what makes you happy."

Writing has always been my very best confidant, power, solace, passion, happiness, and hidden dream. The artist who had lived within me, but never had the chance to blossom, was silenced for decades. But now her voice was returning. The sensitive, bewildered girl inside me who dressed in white and ran in the garden of poetry was almost home, mesmerized by love and affection.

I started taking creative writing classes online at the University of British Columbia. My interest in reading autobiographies, biographies, and memoirs, made me realize that we all have a story to tell, and by doing so, we can reach out and relate globally. First person narrative literature became my best friend. I was not alone, and they talked to me. Gradually, the dreamer was metamorphosing inside me by thinking and writing. I began drafting my own memoir in Farsi-Dari. I announced to Jeb, Yuseuf, and Elias that I was going to write my memoir.

I shared my vision with colleagues and friends. They showed their immense support and belief in me. To my surprise, they honored it with integrity, which made me believe that people know who I really am.

One of my classes was taught by Angela Murrills. Angela Murrills was a writer and food critic. As she was correcting my assignment, she praised me for the style of my writing. I mentioned to her my plan of writing my memoir. She supported me by providing me with her personal email address and suggested that if I ever wanted the story to be looked over, she could help me with it.

When Elias came home for the winter break on the weekend he asked us, "Mom, Dad, there is something that I want to talk to you both about. Can we talk?"

Sweat rushed to my spine, and the volume of my heartbeat forced me to ask, "Is everything okay?"

"Don't worry, Mom. I am fine. It is about my career path." He paused, searched for words to express himself, then finally continued: "I do not want to continue with engineering. I never wanted to become an engineer to begin with." He paused, "I want, I want—I longed to be an actor." He continued, "It has grown within me since grade eleven, but I could not tell you. I didn't say no to engineering because it was important to you, Mom."

I sank into the chair.

Elias continued, "At the Faculty of Engineering—Mom, are you fine?"

"Of course, of course."

He resumed, "One day at the class, the professor defined our future—Mom, your gestures are making me nervous."

"Sorry, Baba Jaan." I withdrew my hand from my chin. He continued, "The professor said, 'One day you guys will graduate, find a job, and get married...' and as the professor was sketching our futures, my life started manifesting before my eyes, and I thought, is that all? I want more from life than just that. I said to myself that I want more, I want to be happy. That was the turning point. The time I spent alone at university made me realize what really makes me happy, and I want to chase it."

One hand covered my mouth while the other scratched my neck. I tried to catch a glimpse of Jeb's face.

"If one day I look back and say to myself, you never tried, I would be really disappointed in myself."

Jeb and I did not know what to say. Jeb leaned back in his chair.

"Come on, Mom, Dad, say something."

Jeb's eyes met mine. It was a lot to take in.

"Let us think about what you've said and we'll talk later," Jeb said, and we all dispersed.

Happiness, freedom, what makes you happy, what your heart desires, chase your dreams, who are you? The very struggles of my own existence suddenly sat before me.

A week later, Jeb and I told Elias, "Go with what your heart desires. Never give up pursuing your dream. We support you, but you should have a backup plan and get a degree."

I stretched my time at the coffee shop with my computer, spending hours of thinking and writing. I translated everything I wrote in Farsi-Dari to English and emailed them to Angela. Angela Murills, who lived on the other side of the globe in the south of France, reached out and fostered the idea that I have a story to tell.

"Parastu, do not accept any rejection. Keep writing and publish your book."

One day, in the middle of my existence, as the sun launched itself to the highest point of the blue sky, after decades of running and facing challenges, I gave birth to my very own self, a free individual.

I opened the computer and wrote:

My name is Parastu Ahang-Mehdawi. I am the daughter of life. I live on the globe. And I am a Writer.

Acknowledgments

I SEE MYSELF AS an author with a voice, and this would not have been possible if I had not manifested this memoir. I could not have done it without the support of so many people that I want to thank now.

When she arrived in Canada, my mother was the age I am right now. She sacrificed so much to build a life free from worry for me.

When I was frozen solid inside, my father became the sun that defrosted the idealistic girl I once was and took me back to the world of literature.

My husband never stopped me from doing or having anything I wished for; this book would not have been possible without his support. And I am who I am right now because of my two sons.

I longed to launch this memoir together with Angela Murrills, an author who believed in me. But she left me, brokenhearted and alone, just when I finished the first half of the book. May she rest in peace.

The *New York Times* author and reviewer for *The Globe* and *Mail*, Marcia Walker, made me travel back to my past and bring those anecdotes to life. As my editor and mentor, she moved me to unearth more and spell it out on paper.

Patricia E Bailey the author of *Beyond Expectations into a World of Possibilities*. Her wisdom and support reached me from the west coast and reminded once again that universe is a one big family.

This memoir's final touches were effected by Susan Gaigher, editor and publishing consultant. Her collaboration, positive attitude, and professional demeanor added much value. Becky Bayne, with her excellence in graphic design, manifested this memoir into book format and distributed it to the world. Her kind voice touched my heart, and I picked her to guide me through the world of publishing. Cynthia Summers's creative photography and Kiersten Armstrong's web design helped me to get on social media to introduce myself to the world.

Frau Bors was the first link in the chain of love in my life, and I will forever stand by her teachings. My deepest respect to all the teachers out there doing wonders and encouraging individual souls to rise.

Finally, to authors all around the globe, thank you for writing books telling your stories and guiding humanity with your wisdom. I reached out to you all and became a writer. I bow down before you.

About the Author

BORN IN KABUL, AFGHANISTAN, Parastu Ahang Mehdawi has been a prose poetry writer since a very young age.

A Quest for Identity is her voice that offers a ladder to the world of literature. She defines herself as a citizen of the world. She is a disciple of human rights. Her message is clear: Stop separating humanity by colour, gender, religion, country, or nationality, and tolerate no war. Parastu's pen dances on the paper when she gets inspired by nature's beauty or is moved to scream by the injustices of the world. Her series of memoirs continues; in the second volume, she narrates her life as a writer and the struggles she faced as the Covid-19 pandemic hit.

Parastu lives in Ontario, Canada, with her family.

⁂

Visit Parastu's website at ParastuaMehdawi.com to join her email list and read more of her writings.

PLEASE CONSIDER LEAVING A review for *A Quest for Identity* on your favorite online retailer! For a self-published author like me, reviews are highly appreciated!

Lightning Source UK Ltd.
Milton Keynes UK
UKHW011940300622
405220UK00008B/163/J